EXHAUSTING
MODERNITY

'The originality of this work is profound. Brennan has produced a totally fresh re-constellation of issues . . . it is one of the most brilliant and illuminating contributions to understanding the contemporary fix I have come across.'

Marilyn Strathern, *University of Cambridge*

'Teresa Brennan's argument is bold and brilliant, bringing Marx and Freud into dialogue after decades of isolation and reviving single-handedly the critical tradition of political economy. The pundits will be surprised: Marx is a woman!'

Susan Buck-Morss, *Cornell University*

'This is stunning . . . Teresa Brennan's scholarship is impeccable and full of compelling analysis, incisive examples, and clear expositions of her arguments . . . it may also be the great spiritual statement against capitalism.'

Kelly Oliver, *SUNY at Stonybrook*

'It is clearly a book of substance and originality. It is vitally useful at this juncture in history to have someone who understands human psychology and Marxian theory comment on the effects of "speeded-up" time in consumption and production . . . it is Teresa Brennan's considerable achievement to analyse the process in all its dimensions.'

Geoffrey Harcourt, *University of Cambridge*

Exhausting Modernity: Grounds for a new economy is a bold, original work on the exhaustion pervading modern capitalism: from environmental collapse to our own depleted psychic lives. The theory offered here explains the ruling dynamics in political economy and psychology today, and what lies behind them. In making its case, *Exhausting Modernity* draws on sources from medieval theology to Freud and Marx.

Exhausting Modernity is essential reading for political and social theorists, philosophers and theologians, economists, and all those interested in the environment.

Teresa Brennan is Schmidt Distinguished Professor of Humanities at Florida Atlantic University.

EXHAUSTING MODERNITY

Grounds for a new economy

Teresa Brennan

London and New York

First published 2000
by Routledge
11 New Fetter Lane, London EC4P 4EE

Simultaneously published in the USA and Canada
by Routledge
29 West 35th Street, New York, NY 10001

Routledge is an imprint of the Taylor & Francis Group

© 2000 Teresa Brennan

Typeset in Photina by
BOOK NOW Ltd
Printed and bound in Great Britain by
Biddles Ltd, Guildford and King's Lynn

British Library Cataloguing in Publication Data
A catalogue record for this book is available
from the British Library

Library of Congress Cataloging-in-Publication Data
Teresa Brennan, 1952–
Exhausting modernity : grounds for a new economy /
Teresa Brennan.
p. cm.
1. Economics–Philosophy. 2. Economics–Religious
aspects. I. Title.
HB72.B72 2000
330′01–dc21
00-034469

ISBN 0-415-23705-X
ISBN 0-415-23706-8

21414068

CONTENTS

CONTENTS

ACKNOWLEDGEMENTS
AND NOTE

My gratitude goes first to Heather Wdowin and Rosslyn
Wuchinich. Their intelligence, kindness under pressure,
ideas and questions in preparing the manuscript made com-
pleting this book as close to enjoyable as that process can be.
My thanks also go to my other colleagues at the Dorothy F.
Schmidt College of Arts and Letters at Florida Atlantic Uni-
versity, particularly Jane Caputi for many discussions and
Henry Abramson for help in transliterating the Aramaic.
I benefited as well from conversations with our visiting
professors: Albena Azmanova, Susan Buck-Morss, Bice
Benvenuto, Drucilla Cornell, Jack Goody, Jeremy Rifkin and
Nawal al-Saadawi. The Afterword to this book sets out its
relation to the economic argument in *History after Lacan*.
Here I would like to thank all of those who helped produce
that initial version of this book, especially Malcolm Bowie,
Sarah Green and Ingrid Scheibler. David Sanders, Julia
Kristeva and Bill Richardson suggested I make the spiritual
argument more explicit. I hope they are not too disappointed
with the results. My final thanks are due to Muna Khogali,
Hannah May and Tony Bruce at Routledge, to Book Now, to
Ptolemaios and other Brennans and, crucially, to the
remarkable Schmidt Family Foundation.

History after Lacan was dedicated to my friend Susan James;
I repeat that dedication here with very much pleasure. I
would also like that dedication to encompass Alice Jardine,

who, like Sue Jones, has also provided a constant point of reference, the best of criticism, and witty encouragement for many years, and to my mother, who has done the same for even longer.

As is usual in a treatise, 'we' in what follows refers to the author and those who, even if they disagree, still follow the argument.

1

INTRODUCTION

The real aim of the devil is not the destruction of holiness but of life. So says Goethe's Mephistopheles, a.k.a. Lucifer, who laments that despite his best endeavours he will not succeed in destroying life's capacity to reproduce itself endlessly. For Augustine too, the devil hates life because he has nothing of his own, no creative power. He tries to make up by capturing life, by pretending that he is what he can never be by possessing the thing he lacks. *Prima facie*, life's opposite of course is not the devil. It is death. But there is a long Christian tradition associating death with diabolic agency. The same tradition holds that death is only overcome at the last judgement, when the devil and death interfere no more with those who share eternal life. Organic decay is at an end. So, apparently, is death.

In fact death can mean more, and worse, than the end of organic decay. In general, after death, an organism re-enters the flow of life, generating other life through its own decomposition. Organic decay is not useless, which is not to say that decay and the smell of corruption are good; just that the force of life is strong enough to gather even these things into itself, so that they re-enter life's cycles. As with orthodox Judaism, the Christian churches once prohibited cremation, and the faithful believed that this was so their bodies could rise again at judgement.[1] When rationalists gauged that, after all, a buried body was likely to have turned to dust by the time of the last judgement, and that cremation was therefore permissible, they overlooked the immediate and

1

non-metaphorical meaning of burial, which is that it allows dead flesh to participate in the struggle with death on the side of life.[2]

I will try to show in this book that modernity is producing a more complete and final form of death. Its victorious economy, capitalism, is turning biodegradable life into a form in which it can generate nothing. Once this is plain, it will also be apparent that judgement, in one sense of that term, is anything but metaphorical. One of the most ancient senses we can give to the idea of 'judgement' is, 'that which rights the balance'.[3] By binding more and more of life in a form in which it cannot reproduce life, capitalism, and a complicit modernity, disturbs an ecological balance. How that balance is righted remains to be determined. But there are now few on the planet who dispute that the balance needs to be corrected in this beleaguered present.

Capitalism is based on the one process which fails to reproduce, or assist the reproduction, of other forms of life. It is based on money and the process of commodification which money represents. As we will see, this process, which is the key to continued capital accumulation, converts living things into dead ones. Capital is pitched against nature in such a way that the opposition between them becomes absolute. So, accordingly, does that between death and life. This is the material sense we can give to the dictum: 'No man can serve two masters. It is either God or Mammon.' The opposition is absolute because Mammon, in the following argument, makes its profit through the steady consumption of nature. Less nature, more Mammon. Less life, more death. In addition, Mammon can only continue to make a profit through the continuous overconsumption of nature; that is to say, capitalism as a system cannot sustain its profit levels and sustain the environment at the same time. By sustaining the environment, I mean allowing nature to replenish at the rate of its depletion for production. Below, I will try to draw out the laws which show that sustaining profit and sustaining the environment are mutually exclusive.

In making this argument I will be relying on Karl Marx. More exactly, I will be applying an argument Marx made about human labour-power to nature. He argued that there was a necessary relation between capitalist profit and the exploitation of labour: because labour gives more than it costs, profit is made. That 'extra' from labour is the source of profit and, for Marx, profit comes from this source and this source alone. But this is true only for capitalism; profit was not made this way in other forms of market. (Let us note at the outset that capitalism is not the same thing as the market.) In my argument, capitalism, unlike some other forms of market economy which replenished the natural environment, exploits nature in the same way it exploits labour. As the manner of this exploitation means that capitalism necessarily depletes and degrades nature, conflict between life, or environmental sustainability, and profit is intensified.

The critical opposition between God, as life, and Mammon has been obscured by the growing sympathy of the Christian churches towards money, a sympathy that has increased steadily since the beginnings of capital accumulation in Europe and the consequent rise of capitalism. When the Catholic church, last century, adopted the Protestant revision of St Paul's dictum that 'money is the root of all evil', it made money innocent in itself. The dictum was changed to: 'the desire for money is the root of all evil'. In other words, money is not the issue. The issue, rather, is human cupidity. But by the following argument, money as such is precisely the problem, together with the process of capital accumulation money represents. The extent of accumulation, and the strength of human cupidity, go hand in hand. The problem here, as with the new interpretation of burial, is that the limits of rational understanding and common sense make certain meanings obscure to the reason of this or that historical period. But while those meanings may be opaque, that does not mean they are beyond logic. The fundamental opposition between God and Mammon has also been obscured by the downgrading of nature in much Christian theology after the thirteenth and fourteenth centuries. This downgrading makes it hard to perceive that life, God and regeneration are on one side, while death, the devil and Mammon are on the other. This idea will be plainer if we consider the principal basis for the church's opposition to usury.

At its simplest, the prohibition on usury (the lending of money for interest) blocked the rise of capitalism, which required substantial accumulations of capital as well as the new industrial technology it acquired centuries later.[4] I have to say here, before going further, that the arguments on usury had a hypocritical cast in terms of how those arguments functioned institutionally. In particular, usury was prohibited and at the same time made possible by anti-semitism and the social exclusion of Jews. Usury was one of a few professions allowed to Jews, who sinned neither in Jewish nor canon law by practising it. But while anti-semitism was tied to the struggle against usury, it was not its cause. Before the eleventh century, the prohibition against usury had been absolute. But from the eleventh to the thirteenth centuries, the practice developed while the church struggled to contain it. Hitherto, it had been possible to make a profit on production, say, by loaning agricultural goods, but not by lending money as such.

Following Aristotle, St Thomas Aquinas observed '*Nummus non parit nummos*' (Money does not reproduce itself).[5] While money can be used as a medium of exchange, and St Thomas believes it was invented for this purpose, it is against nature for money to propagate of its own accord. In St Bonaventure's words: 'In itself and by itself, money does not bear fruit but the fruit comes from elsewhere'.[6] Usury stole time and attempted to make it into the fruit of money, *via* the payment of interest. Usury was also associated with death: 'usurers feed upon cadavers and carcasses when they eat food acquired by usury'.[7]

The battle against usury was lost; capital accumulated. But in between this loss and the rise of modernity, money earned via interest was believed to embody death more than any other thing. After industrial technology is born, this financial form of death is also embodied in commodification. That is to say, my argument on the relation between capitalist profit and its dependence on the exploitation of nature introduces a deathly aspect of the production of commodities on a more widespread level. Compared to the Middle Ages, it is so widespread today that the restrictions against usury read like a forewarning of what is to come. By reworking Marx, we are able to see that the capitalist production of commodities spreads death by turning nature into commodities, without replenishing the life it appropriates in the process. The profit based on this commodification is measured by money: itself, for Marx, the exemplary commodity. As we noted at the outset, the production of commodities binds nature more and more in forms that are not biodegradable, forms incapable of re-entering the lifecycles via the reproduction of their own kind or their organic decay. This argument might re-establish something which was self-evident in the theology of the Middle Ages: namely, that money could not reproduce of itself precisely because its own product was dead rather than living, and only living things could reproduce according to natural law. The understanding of natural law is now too often reduced to human bioethics. In a longer work, I would want to argue that natural law had a much broader compass in the Middle Ages; it was also about nature, and a right relation to nature in which hubris was constrained. But enough for here that in that premodern period the relation between usurious money, death and the devil was clear – as was the opposition of all three to nature. For that matter, the tie between God and nature was also plain. So, accordingly, was the opposition between God and Mammon.

Historically, the devil comes into his own at the time the battle against usury begins in the eleventh century.[8] Until then, he had been associated with the principle of obstruction, perhaps, by Judaism (although the Fall of the angels is recorded in the Jewish Bible), and it is claimed that the devil had less theological significance in Christianity before the year 1000.[9] If that interpretation is correct, then the relation between the devil and the initial accumulation of financial capital is even more clear. Chronologically, they coincide.

While the relation between capital, money and the devil is now obscure, I do not want to absolve the *desire* for money of any responsibility in modernity's trajectory. Initially, it was a Protestant revision that made 'the desire for money' rather than money as such the root of evil. But that does not mean it was wrong. I mentioned earlier that the desire for money is strengthened by the power of capitalism, as the culture of money and commodities. A central argument of this book focuses on the dialectical interaction between desire and the objective existence of a commodified world, which reinforces the desire both for money and for gratifying commodities in general. If I am correct, it should be the case that such desire has increased over time, so much so that it should be anathematized together with interest-bearing money.

To lay the grounds for this argument, we turn now to a fantasy that seems to be inborn in the human psyche, a fantasy which has an antagonism to life at its core. This argument will show that the ingredients of this original fantasy parallel those of St Augustine's account of the devil's Fall, as well as his account of original sin. But before proceeding with it, I should offset any impression that this book is conducted throughout in relation to theology as well as social theory. After this introduction, and the next two chapters on the psyche, the argument progresses through a critical political economy. This is not to disavow the links I have been making between the notion of ecological balance and judgement, or (below) between fantasy and an 'original sin'. On the contrary. As we will see, the facts of a religious *fides historica* (faith based on history) can refer to the psyche, as well as events, and what the political and economic order needs to avoid being or becoming if it is not to reinforce a fantasy which would fade away if left unbolstered. In explicating this fantasy, I rely on Sigmund Freud and Melanie Klein. But I shall begin this explication by returning to Goethe's and Augustine's accounts of the Fall.

In Goethe's story of Faust, Mephistopheles breaks away from the original source of creation in order to contest it. This original source is maternal. Goethe calls her Mother Night. The devil on the other hand is 'Haughty Light', a reference both to his pride and his tie to light, hallucination and deceptive vision. This 'Haughty Light', the devil, breaks away from the Mother but he can never break away from Her being. Lucifer must stay 'tied to bodies'. He can only use his light through the human agency the Mother makes. He is a parasite, dependent on and trapped in the very process of life he seeks to forestall.[10]

But life eludes the devil, with a ceaseless creativity that evades complete prediction, and hence control. That the devil desires control is axiomatic, for he feasts on power and the prospect of power. It is this that leads to his famous sin of pride, *superbia*. The devil's sin of pride has often been misunderstood as something rather magnificent. 'I shall not bend the knee', is his imagined cry.[11] Generations of those who have stood on the side of the oppressed have confused their cry with his. But, as we shall see here, according to Augustine, the devil was prompted by something rather different from the drive for equality and the desire to alleviate suffering. He was driven, very simply, by the desire to be boss. From this desire comes a fantasy from which all paranoia and its attendant miseries are born. In this fantasy, the state of being created by another, and dependent on that other, is interpreted as the state of being controlled. The other or others want to keep you in your place. They created you to feel superior. If not for their ignoble ambition, you could be, well, God. This fantasy founds the psyche. In the fullest sense of the word, it is foundational.

The keystone of this book is the analysis of that foundational fantasy. As I have indicated, in that analysis I draw on Augustine, Freud and Melanie Klein. As I have also indicated, there is a parallel between Augustine's accounts of the Fall and original sin and psychoanalytic, especially Kleinian, accounts of the infant's early life. Both Augustine and Klein make omnipotence and envy central in the analysis of evil and paranoia respectively. Their accounts are remarkably similar, and by joining them we fill in some of the lacunae in both.[12] In addition, the logic of their arguments, when taken together with Freud's, yields a theory of the subject/object distinction, and an account of how it is formed, which is the basis of my economic analysis.

The foundational fantasy is the means whereby the human

7

being comes to conceive itself as the source of all intelligence and all agency. It conceives of the other (other people, the world around it) as objects that are there to serve it, to wait upon its needs without making it wait, to gratify it instantly! When the subject makes the other an object, it simultaneously conceives of itself as a subject. Intelligence and agency are what differentiates a subject from an object. This assumption, that an intelligent subject is counterposed to a world of objects, is critical in how the foundational fantasy is globally enacted. By enactment, I mean the process whereby the fantasy is made real in the social order, rather than the psyche. This brings us to the most radical and simple idea in this book.

A process that is studied in microcosm by psychoanalysis is shown in the following argument to be a process at work in the macrocosmic world of commodities. Psychoanalytic insights and theories might be less pertinent to individual processes than they are to social processes. The impulses (and fantasies in the end are only impulses) described in psychoanalysis might not originate in the individual psyche, but in the broader social order. What I mean by this is not simply the truism that the psyche is socialized. I mean that psychoanalysts have observed social dynamics in miniature, that psychoanalytic thinking is premised on looking down a telescope the wrong way. If omnipotent impulses are 'out there' in the social, they wash through the psyche, especially the infant psyche, which is unshielded from the impact of affects from without; unprotected against, say, anxiety or other energies and feelings which the infant mistakenly takes to be its own. In other words, the affects and impulses pre-exist the infant. We are born into them. But people then, and this is our tragedy, take these impulses to be our own, filtering them through the 'I' or ego developed in the first few months of life. The affect is held in common, but the ego makes up its own story, one which explains why the affects are appropriate to it. Henceforth, the affects become its own. This idea entails that the foundational and omnipotent fantasy I am about to discuss can play itself out at various levels: at the social as well as the individual level, and various gradations in between. At the social level, the omnipotent desire to obliterate creativity and life could be manifest in the process of rendering real others superfluous. At the individual level, the overall omnipotent aim of the foundational fantasy, as it is acted out in the social, might be obscure to individuals but they still partake of it when they are its thoughtless vehicles.

The fantasy is made into reality, as commodities are constructed to serve their human masters, to wait upon them, at the expense of the natural world. These commodities are objects which are willing to be controlled; they are nature transformed into a form in which it cannot reproduce itself, nature directed towards human ends. In the Kleinian infantile fantasy, the mother becomes an obliging object, all matter rather than mind, who will none the less obey the infant's will. Here and elsewhere, the mother correlates with nature. It will become clear that the parallel between the psychoanalytic and theological accounts has been obscured because psychoanalysis focuses on the mother while Christian theology has made all divine agency masculine. But if the correlation between the mother, God and nature is borne in mind, it is easier to see how a process that is studied in microcosm by psychoanalysis is paralleled in the macrocosmic world of commodities. But who is to say which came first here, the fantasy or the social process? Evidently, Augustine, and a few others besides who wrote of the Fall as the origin of the devil's omnipotence, did so long before the rise of capitalism, whose seeds may be a thousand years old but which only makes itself felt substantially in the past three centuries. It is in this time that a modern and profoundly Western economy has made omnipotent fantasies into realities. My argument here is that while the fantasy pre-exists modernity, its force in the social order is intensified by modernity. The modern economy, and any social order in which the religious and other ethical constraints on the fantasy are removed, increases the extent to which that fantasy is acted out socially. Hence it increases the extent of commodification, and accordingly, the significance of money. In turn, the fantasy's social enactment increases its hold over the human psyche and the power of the desires born through that fantasy. In explaining this dialectic, we are drawn first to energetics, then to economics.

By energetics I mean the study of the energetic and affective connections between an individual, other people and the surrounding environment. As we will see below, we have good reason for supposing those energetic connections exist; at the same time, the recognition of those connections has been blunted by the tendency to think in subject/object terms. This tendency is linked to the rise of the interior consciousness, which strengthens its hold in the seventeenth century, and has gathered force since. Premoderns conceived of themselves as energetically and psychically connected with their environment and others in it. Subject/object thought automatically separates the subject from that environment. One can debate whether the birth of the interior consciousness marks modernity, a hard case to sustain because of the evident exceptions to it. I would submit that a better measure would be the uniform denial, in the West, of the transmission of affect that we find in effect from the seventeenth century onwards. Subject/object thinking, in brief, is the other side of thinking in terms of the transmission of affect. A psyche that thinks in subject/object terms denies its connection with 'objects'. The subject is precisely other than the object.

In the modern, western world, human beings are affected by energetic connections between themselves and others, but in general they feel these connections unconsciously. This was not always the case. As the third chapter records, even now in the non-western world, the transmission of energy and affect are often taken for granted and experienced consciously. In the West, it seems that the transmission of affect, while once conscious, is now unconscious, an idea which might lead to a revaluation of Foucault. Foucault's argument that the 'repressed unconscious' was more or less invented would be true, but true at a physical, material level, rather than in terms of intellectual history.

The idea of an energetic connection between the subject, others and the environment dims the subject's preeminence. The subject is palpably not the source of all agency if it is energetically connected to, and hence affected by, its context. The hubris of the modern subject finds this notion unpalatable; this subject clings to the notion that humans are energetically separate; that they are born this way, within a kind of shell that protects and separates them from this world. In fact they have to acquire this shell, which is also called the ego.

We will see that the parallel between the foundational fantasy and the trajectory of modernity is, at one level, the product of energetic connections between the psyche and its surrounding environment. But these connections are neither exact nor uniform. On the one hand, foundational thinking will be strengthened at any historical point where the flow of anxiety (for instance) between people is intensified. On the other hand, it takes a few years for the psychosis at the base of this fantasy to play itself out individually; historically, it has taken four centuries. This paradox will be addressed after the argument turns from energetics to economics.

My economic argument draws on Marx, but a Marx without the subject-centred perspective that flawed his theory. It flawed Marx's theory because it prevented him from perceiving that nature as well as labour is a source of value, and of the energy drawn on in turning living nature into commodities and money. If Marx's labour theory of value is read without its emphasis on the subject, if all natural sources of energy are treated as sources of value, his economic theory takes on a new explanatory force. We will see that it becomes a theory of time and energy, capable of explaining why it is that nature has to be exploited by capital if profit is to be made.

Any alternative economic theory, if it is to be of use, should address the realities of lived experience. There is a gap between lived experience and the modes of rational thought most economic theories assume. This is a world where inertia, exhaustion and the sense of running hard to stay in the same place mark everyday life. They are as much a mark of the present depression as environmental degradation. There is a terrible tiredness around, a sense of having no energy, or of energy departing. In fact one can only understand this experience, and the connections between psychical myths and fantasies and the course of capital, if one takes energy into account. It is because it takes account of energy that this book goes further than existing critiques of hubris. These have a long history in philosophy, a history that also culminates in contemporary critiques of subject-centredness. Subject-centredness refers to the idea that the human being ('the subject') is the foundation of agency and meaning. But because the extant critiques of this notion (Heidegger and Levinas, deep ecology and environmental feminism, for instance) are bereft of any accounts of energetics, their bearing on the lived experience of exhaustion is limited. However, there are partial exceptions. Walter Benjamin wrote of the impact technological shifts have upon human energy, via the physical energetic changes technology unleashed; such changes impacted on the human psyche. Benjamin assumed therefore that there is no absolute barrier between the energy of people and that of the world. In this, he was one of the last of a tradition whose most noteworthy exponent was Spinoza.[13] Spinoza insisted that all things were energetically connected; he equated God and Nature, and he did so in the context of the most radical critique of hubris written so far. As we will see, he is the anti-foundational thinker *par excellence*. He may also be closer to medieval theology than traditional bifurcations between Judaism and Christianity allow.[14]

In addition to addressing the energy crises at the personal as well as the macro-structural level, my argument also addresses the increasing anxiety that accompanies any delay, in love or business, and the frustration occasioned by having to wait. Our world hates waiting. It wants and desires it now (whatever it is). In the erstwhile Eastern block, all those photos of all those queues signaled the end of an era. The message was this: in communist states, things are hard to get and, what is worse, you have to wait to get them. In the developed world, the North, the main promise of new and old products alike is that they will save you waiting; indeed, they will wait on you. They will come to you as fast as pizzas;

they are at your service, now if not forever. Provided credit is good.

This book is organized in three parts: the first on the psyche, the second on economics, the third on the polity. In sum: Part I outlines how the self-contained ego comes into being, and hubris along with it. It does so in two ways. The first way is through a synthesis of various psychoanalytic theories (Freud, Klein and Lacan), which reveals how the individual is constructed as separate from the mother and the environment more broadly. The second is through a brief history that shows how conceiving of human beings as self-contained individuals is a modern idea, and very probably a Western prejudice. In Part II, we also see that time is made over in favour of an ever-increasing spatial expansion. In addition, I argue that the ever-increasing scale, the ever-expanding scope of capital is as necessary to capital's profit as its exploitation of nature, and that opposition to this exploitation should go hand in hand with opposing the large scope of its operations. Part III adumbrates a different under-standing of historical time. The sense of the significance of time is in the air. It is attested to not only by Heidegger and Derrida, but by the plethora of lay books on physics available today. But physics is not the only science of time. Economics is another such science. What this book is about, in the end, is the connection between the time of economics and the time of physics, for this is the key to the inertia that has to be overcome in daily survival. In the end, we will see too that personal inertia is directly tied to global entropy, via the proliferation of commodities. Inertia is precisely not a personal problem, but an effect of the speeding up of the world. Inertia, energy, time and speed are all interwoven in the domain of physics which, as Hawking has shown us, is a science of time. Time is the common factor in the pheno-mena pointed to so far: not for nothing do we speak of waiting time; time is also a dimension of speed, and time is what one loses through inertia. On this basis, I attempt to explain the paradox noted above: the temporal disjunction between the subjective and historical incidence of the foundational fantasy.

Part III also outlines an alternative economic politics, together with a basis for synthesizing diverse oppositional trends. I develop this alternative elsewhere.[15] Here I only indicate that in that alternative (some) small-scale businesses and small-scope enterprises are seen as a natural source of opposition to large-scale capital. It is a middle way in that it seeks to find common ground for the various groups and tendencies that – taken together – make up the opposition to the current course of humankind.

These groups range from the Green movement, including both its spiritual and its socialist tendencies, to the anti-imperialist and workers' movements, to the sexual politics movements, to the growing opposition in the churches to capitalism, and to alternative cultures. Taken together, they make up a formidable force. But their power as an opposition has been weakened by the lack of a common analysis. This lack has been fostered by what Rorty sees as a kind of dereliction of duty on the part of many academic critics.[16] These critics, at precisely the historical point where we confront a totalizing process in practice, have chosen to oppose it by saying that we cannot totalize in theory. This means that only the 'progressives' (the proponents of the unfortunate idea that large-scale industrialization has brought us progress), only these intellectuals outline general philosophical theories. A rigorous general theory of why we witness deterioration rather than progress has been absent, but it is exactly this general theory that is needed now. In what follows, I have tried to outline a theory of this kind.

However, as perhaps I have indicated, my point of departure is at least informed by the current turn in academic critical and social theory: the critique of foundationalism begun by Heidegger. Everything criticized under the rubric of 'foundationalism' depends on the assumption that the human being is the privileged origin of meaning, intelligence and truth. This is why I have borrowed the term 'foundational' to describe the fantasy. But I stress that using the term foundational does not mean that there are no 'foundations'. (In this I differ from Derrida, who extends Heidegger's critique.) There is a difference between the idea that the human being is not the source of meaning, and the assumption that there is no meaning at all. There is also a difference between the illusory yet material foundations constructed in the name of the fantasy (human autonomy and will) and the natural, generative foundations that sustain life.

These natural foundations are covered over as the fantasy is reinforced historically and acted out technologically through the proliferation of commodities, and the rise of money as the measure of all things. In the first instance, the foundational fantasy will become clearer not through concentrating on the psychical fantasies described in existing psychoanalytic theories, but through considering the desires encapsulated in consumer goods, or commodities: things that are socially produced for monetary exchange and psychically desired. Let us start with the desire for instant gratification, described by Freud, and realized in a proliferation of commodities.

Notes

1 In part, the Orthodox Jewish prohibition on cremation also devolves from belief in the physical resurrection of the body. On the other hand, the process of organic decay was certainly known to the Ancients, who allowed for the decay of the flesh in a temporary burial before the bones were removed and interred. Ancient Jewish death rituals are the topic of the Talmudic tractate *Semahot*. See also Sylvie Ann Goldberg, *Crossing the Jabbok: Illness and Death in Sixteenth through Nineteenth Century Prague*, tr. Carol Cosman (Berkeley, CA: University of California Press, 1996).

2 Jane Caputi made me reconsider my hitherto overly homogenous understanding of death. Her argument on how death and decay are symbolized positively as well as negatively in relation to symbolic and mythical representations of the maternal is outlined in her paper, 'On the Lap of Necessity' (*Hypatia*, forthcoming). The understanding that death and decay have life-giving properties is very much at the heart of Hasidic theodicy. This is discussed in greater detail in the classic eighteenth century Hasidic work of Rabbi Shneur Zalman of Liadi, *Tanya* (1796). The life-giving properties of death and (as?) organic decay are also discussed in a work by the founder of

Hasidism, Rabbi Israel Baal Shem, 'The Bad is a Throne for the Good', cited in Nehemia Polen, *The Holy Fire: The Teachings of Rabbi Kalonimus Kalman Shapia, the Rebbe of the Warsaw Ghetto* (Northvale, NJ: Jason Aronson, 1994), p. 122. Indeed the distinction I draw between death as decay and death as permanently destructive is basic to centuries-old Hassidism. It is discussed in Henry Abramson, 'The Esh Kodesh of Rabbi Kalonimus Kalmish Shapiro: A Hasidic Treatise on Communal Trauma from the Holocaust', in *Transcultural Psychiatry*, vol. 37 (3), forthcoming (Montreal, 2000).

3   Strictly, rendering justice is the act of righting the balance, while judgement is both the determination of the means for righting the balance, as well as the process itself. *Contra* Heidegger, I would argue that the idea of justice – and judgement – as natural processes is implicit in Anaximander's fragment: 'some other infinite [apeiron] nature, from which come into being all the heavens and the worlds in them. The source of coming-to-be for existing things is that into which destruction, too, happens, "according to necessity; for they pay penalty and retribution to each other for their injustice according to the assessment of Time".' The first half-sentence, as reported, may be about a creative source; that is to say, it is a statement about cosmogony. The second sentence can be interpreted as meaning, or as also meaning, that the generation of life is the organic decay of other life; and existing things too are subject to the same organic decay. The quotation within Anaximander's fragment could also mean that all living things are necessarily bound to one another, and those living things that had gone before them, in their own birth and growth, or coming-to-be. This would mean that 'justice' was a matter of taking no more than you needed to live, and live so that you were able to make the specific contribution to life of which you were capable. G. S. Kirk, J. E. Raven and M. Schofield (eds. and trs.) *The Presocratic Philosophers: A Critical History with a Selection of Texts*, second edition (Cambridge: Cambridge University Press, 1983), p. 118. Heidegger criticizes the naturalist readings of the fragment. He notes only to reject the possible interpretation of it as a statement about nature. (Heidegger aside, the existence of a general category of nature until after Anaximander's time is disputed. Kirk *et al.*, pp. 102–3*n*.) Instead Heidegger wants the fragment to be a statement about being. Specifically, he reads it in terms of how Being, as presence, requires withdrawal. In this, he is looking for a sphere beyond either a mechanistic understanding of nature on the one

hand, or metaphysics on the other. But he looks for this sphere in the abstract, as do all who follow the flight from the flesh into metaphor. M. Heidegger, *Early Greek Thinking: The Dawn of Western Philosophy*, tr. David Ferrell Krell and Frank A. Capuzzi (San Francisco: Harper and Row, 1984), p. 21.

4 Jacques Le Goff, *Your Money or Your Life: Economy and Religion in the Middle Ages* (New York: Zone Books, 1998). This introductory discussion of usury is substantially indebted to Le Goff. Also see Karl Marx, *Capital* [1894], 3 vols. (Moscow: Progress Publishers, 1971).

5 Moreover, and remembering that justice, like judgement, is a matter of balance, we can note St Thomas's remark that 'making a charge for lending money is *unjust* in itself, for one party sells the other something non-existent, and this obviously sets up an *inequality* which is contrary to *justice*'. Thomas Aquinas, *Summa Theologia* [1266–9], ed. and tr. T. McDermott as *Summa Theologica: A Concise Translation* (Westminster, MD: Christian Classics, 1989) IIa, 11ae.

6 Le Goff, *Your Money*, p. 29.

7 Ibid., pp. 56–7. Le Goff is quoting Jacques de Vitry.

8 By the time the battle is over, the prospect of damnation and the practice of usury have been divorced due to Pope Gregory's reforms concerning purgatory. When the usurer can go to purgatory, the fear of hell is removed. As Le Goff puts it, with the idea of purgatory, it is possible to have riches and paradise, because it is possible to repent for ill-gotten riches in purgatory. Before that, the choices had been stark – ever since the church's abolition of the doctrine of reincarnation at the fourth-century Council of Nicaea.

9 It is currently fashionable to believe that Satan was not a figure of evil in Judaism and that, as a figure of evil, he is a Christian invention. It is certainly true that the projection of Satan or satanic purposes onto others has accompanied Christian persecution, and has not marred Judaism. But while the representations of Satan in the Jewish Bible and the Talmud are complex, and while it is also the case that in the biblical Book of Job Satan is subservient to and constrained by God in his capacity as tempter, it is not the case that there is no 'fallen one' in the Jewish Bible, nor any notion of Satan as evil in Judaism. The Talmud considers Satan, the desire to do evil, and the Angel of Death to be one and the same. ('Amar Reish Lakish: hu satan hu yetser hu-ra hu malakh ha-mavet', *Bava Batra*, folio 17a.) The Fall of the angels is referred to perhaps by Judaism in the Book of Genesis (6: 4): 'and the fallen ones [*elohim*] were on the earth in

those days', although the rabbinic commentators struggle with 'the fallen ones' and 'the sons of *elohim*'.

10 Goethe, *Faust*, part 1, scene 3.

11 Milton, *Paradise Lost*, Book 1, lines 11–12.

12 The problem with the parallel between Melanie Klein's theory about the innateness of envy and its effects, and St Augustine's account of the Fall (even though he describes envy in the crib) is that *invidia* leads to the Fall of the angels, not of Man. The Fall of Man is occasioned by biting the apple at the behest of the tempting serpent, a metaphor which is traditionally interpreted as tasting the tree of knowledge. In a great paper, Marco Pallis confesses how he wondered as a child how it was that there were two trees in the garden of Eden: the tree of knowledge and the tree of life. In adult life, having been one of the fortunate ones who grow in wisdom, he realized that there was only one tree. Before the Fall, the moment of separation, it was the tree of life. From the perspective of separation, it was the tree of knowledge of good and evil. In other words, when one partakes fully of life, when one is in the state of complete union with God, there is no knowledge of good and evil because there is no evil. Marco Pallis, 'Is There a Problem of Evil?' in *The Sword of Gnosis* (ed.) Jacob Needleman (Baltimore: Penguin Books, 1974). But to return to the two Falls, that of the angels and that of Man: if these were somehow one Fall, then the birth of envy, and of knowledge as the will to power in the sense of control, would be coincident, as indeed they are in Melanie Klein's account of infancy. Theologically, however, the Fall of the angels antedates that of Man. The timing is wrong, but then there may be a resolution through more understanding of the nature of time; ultimately, it is to the analysis of time that this book tends.

13 For the most sensitive and scholarly work in English on Benjamin, see Susan Buck-Morss's remarkable reconstruction of Benjamin's unpublished Arcades Project: *The Dialectics of Seeing: Walter Benjamin and the Arcades Project* (Cambridge, MA: The MIT Press, 1989).

14 'Making coins give birth to more coins . . . is that not a sin *against nature*? Were theologians not saying, especially since the "naturalist" twelfth century, *"Natura, id est Deus"* (Nature, that is to say, God)?' Le Goff, *Your Money*, p. 31.

15 T. Brennan, *Your Money or Your Life: The Real Third Way* (forthcoming). In tribute, I have borrowed the translator's title for Le Goff's book, published in French as *La bourse et la vie: economie et religion au Moyen Age*, Paris: Hatchette, 1986.

16 Richard Rorty, *Philosophy and Social Hope* (New York: Penguin USA, 2000).

Part I

PSYCHE

2

THE FOUNDATIONAL
FANTASY

The vending machine that provides instantly upon the insertion of a coin, the fast-food establishment that promises no delay, the internet connection that promises immediate access, the bank card that advertises itself as the one that does away with the need to stand in a queue: all promise the abolition of waiting time. Yet a little reflection shows that commodities cater to more than a desire for instant gratification. They are also marked by an attitude of appealing availability: the 'I'm here for you' message signified by the trolley at the airport that asks you to 'rent me', or the advertisement that once asked you to 'fly me'. These appealing items are akin to those that promise service, such as the credit card that delivers the object of desire to your door. 'Pick up the phone; we come to you.' More than the abolition of waiting time is offered here; one will also be waited upon. And if the promise of service appeals to a desire for domination and control, it has to be noted that the illusion of control is also provided by vending machines and their ilk. The consumer is catered to via the fantasy of direction with minimal effort, even none at all. In this connection, the car is an exemplary commodity. It pollutes the surrounding environment. At the same time, it provides mobility without much activity to a passive director. Consumers make it happen. All they need is money.

In proposing that the desires encapsulated in commodities embody a foundational fantasy I am proposing that we treat the commodity as an expression of that fantasy, a means of fulfilling it. But immediately this proposition raises two problems. The first is that the desires encapsulated in commodities do not tally exactly with any existing account of a psychical fantasy. The second problem of course is demonstrating that the fantasy expressed in commodities is in fact foundational.

We are not entirely in a void when it comes to considering these problems. While there is no extant account which tallies precisely with the psychical fantasy I am assuming commodities encapsulate, a synthetic reading of certain psychoanalytic theories will provide one. In addition, that synthetic reading coheres because it makes central the psychical fantasies Klein describes about the mother's body. This focus on Klein also reveals just what objectification, and with it the subject/object distinction, entails. But Freud comes first.

Persistently, consumer goods appeal through visual media. This, together with the desire for instant gratification these commodities 'as consumer goods' encapsulate, directs us to Freud's pleasure principle. Freud's pleasure principle, more strictly his principle of *Unlust* or unpleasure as he first defined it, is about a hallucinatory visual world where instant gratification is paramount. It is also about how psychical reality as distinct from 'material reality' comes into being.[1] When the longed-for object (initially the breast or mother) is not present it is hallucinated in its absence. This hallucination founds psychical reality; the breast is present in the imagination, but not present in the material here and now. The act of hallucination provides instant gratification, but the satisfaction it affords is only short-term. For the breast is longed for because the infant is hungry, and the hallucination cannot appease the unpleasure of the need for food. In other words, unpleasure is due to the tension of need. Any need (to eat, urinate, defecate, ejaculate) increases quantitatively, and pleasure is felt when the need is relieved. A hallucinated breast does not of itself relieve the need. Indeed it ultimately leads to more unpleasure, in that it generates motor excitations it cannot dispel; the expected satisfaction that accompanies the hallucination gears the body up, but the energy amassed through this excitement cannot be relieved, any more than the original need itself.[2]

It should be clear that Freud's (un)pleasure principle is an economic or quantitative principle: it is about the quantitative build-up of tension or need. In Freud's own terms, it is a matter of psychical economy, loosely based in Fechner's psychophysics.[3] The economic or quantitative physical aspects of Freud's theory of the pleasure principle are frequently criticized. Its descriptive aspects are more generally accepted; few commentators have problems with the notion of instant gratification, or with that of visual hallucination. Yet it is the fact that Freud had a reference point in physics, even if it was the wrong reference point, that will be of most use in the long run.

Moreover, if one reconsiders the desires implicit in commodities, it will be plain that while the pleasure principle accords with the desire for instant gratification that they express, and with their visual presentation in various media, it does not account for the other desires revealed in their design, namely: the desire to be waited upon; the desire to believe one is the source of agency who makes it happen; the desire to dominate and control the other who is active in providing, but whose activity is controlled by a relatively passive director, and the aggressive desire towards the other, if we take pollution as evidence of aggression.

The last-named desire returns us to Klein. In her theory, the infant desires to spoil and poison the breast (and the mother) with its excrement. In discussing the infant's desires in Klein's theory, I should repeat the brief caveat on the notion that 'the infant' is the sole culprit when it comes to pinpointing the origin of the aggressive desires under discussion. 'The infant' is always that origin for Klein, although we will see later that the question of culpability is more complicated, as is the idea that the target of all this aggression is simply 'the mother'. But, for the time being, I shall continue to write in terms of infants and mothers. As well as desiring to poison, the infant also desires to devour and fragment the mother's body. 'Cutting up' the mother's body is a recurrent theme in Klein's analyses of small children. She ties this cutting impulse to the drive for knowledge: the urge to get inside, grasp and in this sense understand what is hidden, and in the process destroy it.[4]

For Klein, the desires to poison, devour, dismember and to know through dismembering are prompted by three inter-related forces. The first is the strength of the death drive working within. The second is the envy of the creativeness embodied in the mother and mother's breast. The third is greed. One wants to devour the entire breast, and beyond that, the mother's body. While the death drive, envy and greed motivate these fantasmatic attacks on the breast, they also lead to a fear of retaliation. The fear is that the aggressed breast will respond in kind; this fear results in what Klein terms the paranoid-schizoid position. It is paranoid because the infant projects its own aggressive desires onto the other, and the retaliation it fears (being cut up, poisoned, devoured) mirrors its own desires. It is schizoid because this paranoid projection involves a splitting both of the ego and of the other. For to deal with its dependence on the breast as the source of life, and its simultaneous fantasy that the breast is out to get it, the infant splits: there is a 'good' breast and a 'bad' one. Yet because the badness the infant fears origi-nates within itself, the splitting of the other presupposes and perpetuates a splitting of the ego. This splitting is potentially persecutory. When the ego projects its aggression onto the other, it enters into a dialectic of paranoia and persecution, in which, imagining that the other is out to get it, it persecutes the other in turn. Whenever it feels guilt over the damage done in its fantasy (or reality) that guilt only increases its need to project its bad feeling (guilt in this case) onto the other, which is why there is a tendency to attack again (and again) the person one has already harmed.[5]

The ego, by depositing its own aggressive desires in the other, impoverishes itself by the splitting, and the repres-sion or 'denial' that this entails. The psyche can only recover its full potential by reclaiming that which has been cast out. This reclamation, when it occurs, can lead to depression: the recognition that the erstwhile projected badness lies within. It may also lead to reparation: the attempt to repair the damage done in fantasy;[6] this reparation is manifest in creativeness or, I think, creative labour: both means to integrating a psyche felt to be in pieces. Leaving that hopeful note aside: it is important to add that the extent of the splitting, are of the poisoning, devouring, dismembering fantasies that accompany splitting, is mediated by anxiety. For Klein, anxiety derives from the death drive working within. In the last analysis, she posits that the strength of the death drive, and envy, are innate. Moreover, Klein's account of the splitting process presupposes a psychical fantasy which has no direct correspondence with reality (the breast is not really cut up, etc.). It is a psychical fantasy, and clearly not a consequence of the infant's actual social environment or social events.

Thus far, we have a theory that accounts for the desire to poison, or, in commodity terms, the desire to pollute. We also have some elements of a theory that accounts for the desire to dominate and control (in so far as the desire to get inside, cut up, devour and so on involves control and domination). It remains to tie this theory to the instant hallucinatory gratification embodied in the pleasure principle, and the desire to be waited upon from an inactive though authoritative position, before we have a full account of objectification. Here Klein's analysis of envy provides an indirect clue.

> Though superficially [envy] may manifest itself as a coveting of the prestige, wealth and power which others have attained, its actual aim is creativeness. The capacity to give and preserve life is felt as the greatest gift, and therefore creativeness becomes the deepest cause for envy. The spoiling of creativity implied in envy is illustrated in Milton's *Paradise Lost*, where Satan, envious of God, decides to become the usurper of Heaven. Fallen, he and his other fallen angels build Hell as a rival to Heaven, and becomes the destructive force which attempts to destroy what God creates. This theological idea seems to come down from St Augustine, who describes Life as a creative force opposed to Envy, a destructive force.[7]

This passage is interesting because it points out, although it does so obliquely, that envy superficially focuses on attributes or possessions, rather than the creative force which may (or may not) result in them. The quotation from Klein also points out that envy will attempt to rival that which it envies, and that it will do so by constructing an alternative. More generally, Klein's analysis of envy in the essay from which the above quotation comes shows that while envious motivations are readily recognizable in destructiveness or calumny, they are less recognizable, although present, in denial. This is the form of denial which simply ignores or forgets that which is displeasing to the ego. It is present in the denial of the labour involved in creativity. I add that we recognize it where creativity is seen as accidental, or where it is attributed to a lucky circumstance or an unearned possession.

Let us add to these observations a notion that is best elaborated by Freud – reversal into the opposite. This is the idea that the infant, or small child, imagines the reversal of the actual state of affairs, and imagines that the mother is a dependent infant.[8] In reversing the passive experiences of childhood into active ones in his play with a cotton-reel, Freud's grandson not only masters the mother's absence and introduces himself to deathly repetition,[9] nor does he only, if simultaneously, enter the world of language through the mother's absence that forces him to 'call' or cry out in fledgling words. He also makes the mother into a fantasized small child which he controls, a child which is also an inanimate thing.

If the notion of the reversal of the original state of affairs is made central, rather than the incidental aside it was for Freud, it has the advantage that it reconciles otherwise diverse findings. When realities are seen in terms of their opposites, the fact of nurturance and the means to grow becomes a threat to narcissism; it establishes the reality of dependence. From this perspective, the envy of the mother's breast is the resentment of that dependence, and the reason why nurturance, or love, or protection, or assistance, are interpreted as assertions of superiority, power, and control.

'Only saints are sufficiently detached from the deepest of the common passions to avoid the aggressive reactions to charity.'[10] There is a related, if less relevant, offshoot of the reversal of the original state of affairs into its opposite, an offshoot which we might usefully term 'imitating the original', in which rivalry with the original is clearly apparent. The child imitates the mother; the commodity, harking back to this chapter's point of departure, is often an imitation of the original.[11] Stores and supermarkets stock artificial orange drink in orange-shaped containers with green leaves. Late night television shows the *The Stepford Wives*, which is all about constructing a reliable and completely controllable imitation of the original wife and mother, and *Star Trek II*, where 'Project Genesis' shows us humans reinventing the entire process of creation.

The idea that we live in a culture of *simulacra* is developed by Baudrillard[12] whose study of America shows how much of its culture is a copy of a copy, and sometimes of yet another copy. In Baudrillard's world of hyper-real, more real than real copies, the disappearance of the distinction between the original and the imitation is due to the inability to locate an origin or referent for meaning.[13] Yet in today's *Zeitgeist* what is lost, in fact explicitly rejected, is any notion of an original; an original is a notion of a foundation, hence suspect. I am challenging this suspicion by focusing on the mother's body, which, like the natural order of which it is part, is an origin before the foundation.

It is one thing to say, with Lévi-Strauss and post-structuralists after him, that there is 'no concept of nature outside of culture'. It is another to say that there is no nature. Unfortunately, these different levels of observation are often conflated, as we shall see. But keeping to the main thread: the tendency to look at realities in terms of their opposites is manifest at another level, which will explain the desire to be waited upon. Originally, the infant is perforce passive, and dependent on the mother's activity for survival. Yet it would be consistent with a fantasmatic reversal of the original state of affairs if the infant were to correlate its actual dependent reality with the fantasy of control through imagining that the mother's activity takes place at its behest. The infant does not wait upon the mother; the mother waits upon it. It is precisely this fantasy that is catered to by the commodities with which we began. But a little of reality lingers on in the association between passivity and luxury, which recognizes that it is not the passive controller, or 'the infant', who labours. At the same time, the labour or activity involved in fulfilling the fantasy is denied in so far as its intelligence is denied. In fantasy, the mental direction and design of what labour effects is appropriated, only the manual activity is left out. Thus the mental whim and control is the infant's. The work goes elsewhere.

The split occasioned by this fantasy prefigures a deeper dualism between mind and body, in which direction or agency is seen as mental and mindful, while activity, paradoxically, is viewed as something that lacks intelligence. By an ineluctable logic, the activity of women as mothers is presented as passive. In fantasy, it lacks a will of its own; it is directed from without. And because direction is too readily confused with a will of one's own, this denial can be extended readily to living nature overall. In this connection, it is worth noting that the oft-repeated association of women and nature can be explained not by what women and nature have in common, but by the similar fantasmatic denial imposed upon both of them. In the case of women, it is one's will that is denied. In the case of living nature, its own inherent direction is disregarded.[14]

That creativeness is not viewed as intelligent or directed activity is consistent with envy's predilection to focus on creativity as the possession of certain attributes, rather than as a force in itself. Creativeness is seen less as what one does, than what one has. Or, to say a similar thing differently, the dialectics of envy conduct themselves at the level of images. It is appropriate that the word envy is derived from the Latin verb *videre*: the derivation signals the tie between the concept of envy and visualization.[15] What matters is the appearance of the thing, rather than the process of which it is part.

To say that what is envied is the mother's possession of

the breast is to work already within the terms of envy, which are those of possessions, things, appearances, discrete entities, separable and separate from an ongoing process. Which brings us to the crux of the matter. While a fantasy of controlling the breast cannot survive at the level of feeling (pain or pleasure), it can survive at the literally imaginary level of hallucination. In fact, the controlling fantasy can be perpetuated through hallucinations, and this ability to perpetuate it must contribute to the addiction to the pleasure in hallucination. In other words, by this account, the fantasy of controlling the breast and the act of hallucination are one and the same, which means that the amazing visual power of hallucination is tied to a desire for omnipotence from the outset.[16]

Of course feelings of omnipotence, for Freud, are infantile in origin, and also tied to narcissism. But while there has been some discussion of how it is that narcissism can only come into being through fantasy or hallucination, the other side of this issue, which is how it is that hallucination is by nature an omnipotent or narcissistic act, has not been discussed.[17] It is one thing to concentrate on how it is that the subject's sense of itself as a separate being is inextricably linked to narcissism; that is to say, that it is only by the narcissistic act of fantasizing about its own body or circumference that it establishes its separate self. It is another to think about how the narcissism involved is also, and simultaneously, an omnipotent fantasy about controlling the other. For to establish itself as separate, the subject has to have something to be separate from.

But, by this account, the thing the subject is separate from is the breast or mother it imagines as available to it, subject to it, and towards whom it feels the aggressive desires that lead in turn to paranoia. Moreover, in the omnipotent act of hallucinating a breast it controls, the nascent subject separates and gives priority to its own visual capacity for imagination over its other senses. It is this visual capacity that allows one to imagine that things are other than they are; it is this capacity that enables one to focus on the distinctiveness of entities other than oneself, rather than the senses or feelings that connect one with those others; it is this capacity that enables the subject to believe in (and even achieve) a situation where mental design and direction can be divorced from bodily action. In my theory's terms, the tie between hallucination and envy means that the very act of hallucination can never be neutral. In St Augustine's imagery, if the fallen angel of light (Lucifer: *lux* = light, *ferre* = bring) fell because of envy there is no reason for supposing that he lost his power of light altogether; rather, in the act of hallucination, light becomes actively distorted and re-directed as an imaginary and necessarily envious vision.

As noted at the outset, there is a striking similarity between Augustine's account of the Fall and Melanie Klein's account of the infant psyche (as Klein herself seems aware). But the similarity is obscured by any reading that valorizes Lucifer's pride. The best-known example here is Hannah Arendt, who sees in Lucifer 'that *superbia* of which only the best are capable: they don't want to serve God but to be like Him'.[18] They want, Arendt says, to be the equal of any other that there is. But Augustine himself makes it plain that *superbia* is much closer to what today would be called omnipotence: the condition of denying others' rights or even the separate existence of others in favour of the wish to dominate and control them.

This is what Augustine actually says of *superbia*. '(P)ride in its perversity apes God. It abhors equality with other men under Him; but, instead of His rule, it seeks to impose a rule of its own upon its equals.'[19] Similarly, what makes the earthly city unheavenly is that 'the princes and the nations it subdues are ruled by the love of ruling'.[20] There is a lust for domination in them, a direct reflection of the devil's wish to assert omnipotence by dominating his equals. Stressing this is not to say that Augustine is an equalitarian, (although Kristeva, amongst others, makes a case for an equalitarian ethic in Christianity as such); the point is that Augustine distinguished between service and domination, obligation and control. All human beings were obliged equally to serve God and love one another in service. The methods of service vary, but all are equal in their *obligation*, whether it is to serve or to obey, and all are equal before God.[21]

Even if one wishes not to pass so lightly over Augustine's feudalism, the fact remains that the wish to dominate is not the same as the wish for equality. The way in which the two wishes are the same for the devil will be plainer through drawing out how, in Augustine's account of the Fall, *superbia* is allied with *invidia* or envy. For Augustine they cannot be separated, as he makes plain in his *Confessions*. Thus when he wonders how he might have sinned in infancy, he asks whether he might have done so

> by falling into a rage against my nurses and parents and many other discreet persons, and by endeavouring to strike and hurt them as much as I could, whensoever they did not punctually obey me? [*non ad nutum voluntatis obtemperantibus feriendo nocere niti quantum potest . . .*] Though he ought not to be said to be obeyed, who is but obeyed to his destruction. If so, it is the weakness of an infant's body which is innocent, whereas the mind is not innocent.
>
> Myself have seen and observed some little child, who could not speak, yet he all in an envious kind of wrath, looking pale, with a bitter countenance upon his foster-brother. And who is ignorant of this?[22]

The rage at not being punctually obeyed is now termed omnipotent rage. It sits alongside envy in infancy. As in infancy, so in the Fall. *Invidia* and pride in concert cause Lucifer to act as he does. *Invidia* is the deadliest of the seven deadly sins because it attempts to destroy the source of life and goodness itself. It is the sin that bites the hand that feeds it, and by this biting, it robs even its doers of what they need in order to survive. Here again, *invidia* and *superbia* are intertwined. For closely related to, in fact another aspect of, the envy that bites the hand is pride, as an omnipotent denial of dependence. 'It is to this basic denial of dependence, and so of gratitude, that Augustine will point, in politics, in thought, in religion.'[23] We can add that the denial is effected – in politics – by those who dispute God's claims by ruling through domination. It is effected in thought by those who do not reflect on the conditions of their ability to think; in religion, in any heresy that downplays God's role in relation to creation, a recurrent theme in Augustine's dissection of paganism.

In the last analysis, it is a denial of dependence, I think, on life and the capacity to generate life. As we have seen, envy and Diabolus are synonyms often for death, reminding us that for Augustine the real struggle is between life and death, and that it is death that Jesus is meant to conquer. That life itself is at issue also emerges through a little reflection on Augustine's understanding of the good and the envious. The evil regard the good with 'diabolical, envious hatred . . . for no other reason than they are good while themselves are evil.'[24] But goodness, like life, can be shared without diminishing the stock of goodness of those who already have it. There is something in evil which operates according to a zero-sum principle. If I have it, you may not. My life, your death. The essence of envy seems to be exactly that what the one has the other loses, although envy realizes that goodness, by being shared, simply generates more of itself.[25] This is the same principle that governs the proliferation of life. Lucifer then, by this interpretation, is envious of God's capacity to create life, which he interprets in terms of power: the power to make, the power not to do so.

Having interpreted God's motivation as power (an interpretation that dogs subsequent theology of evil), Lucifer wants this power for himself. *Superbia*, in other words, is the desire for power over the other, and it cannot be divorced from a comparative view of that other, in which what the other has, and the self does not, is envied. Envious and proud, Lucifer falls, and with his fellow fallen angels, attempts to build hell as a rival to heaven. His ambition is to ape the heavenly city, founded on earth through Abel, by the construction of the earthly city, whose founder is the rivalrous Cain. Envy is not only about possession. It is about rivalry. The other is seen as possessing something that gives them an edge. It is the edge, more than the possession, that is resented.

Rivalry is the wish to reverse positions. Lucifer does not

only wish to be equal with God, he wishes to be God. Were Lucifer to be successful in his ambition, then from Lucifer's standpoint, God would be left with the options of filling Lucifer's recently vacated place, or disappearing altogether (not that we should imagine God has been much exercised over the question).

In sum, power over the other, rather than the striving to be equal, is the hallmark of *superbia* for Augustine. This is why the devil's sin of pride is misunderstood when it is seen as something that 'brings out the best' as Arendt put it.[26] *Superbia* is rather omnipotence, the 'lust to dominate' by taking the other's right. But there is a problem, not explicitly resolved by St Augustine, although his philosophy lends itself to a resolution. The problem is this: why does Lucifer interpret the capacity to create as power over others? This question takes us back to Klein, who gives us more of an answer.

In part Klein gives us a more explicit answer because the very business of analysis is always a question of the inter-pretation of fantasies, of their projection and the distortions they effect. Reading Augustine through Klein, we might say that the devil interprets God's creativity as power and control because he projects his own motivations onto God. He fears that God will do to him what he wishes to do to God. To venture into the territory of fears and motivations is to find not only that Klein describes them in terms that parallel Augustine's, but that she also helps us account for the confusion between domination and creativity in other ways. The object of her analysis, of course, is not the devil and the Fall, but the infant and its fantasies. And the aim of the envious infant is not the creativity of God the father but of the mother. It is the dependence on the mother and the mother's creativity that the infant denies. It denies both because of its envy of that creativity and its rage at that dependence. At the outset then we can note that there is already a denial at work in Augustine's account: the creative source of life is figured as paternal.[27] A paternal source of creation is already suspect; it may have already committed acts of expropriation and domination. The denial of creativity and dependence begins here with the denial of the mother, and all patriarchal – using the word for once in its strict sense – systems of thought invite a further denial, even diabolic denial, by a logic they themselves inaugurate. On the other hand, if we read Klein through Augustine, her theory takes on a coherence it otherwise lacks. Especially when buttressed by a little Freud, it becomes a coherent account of an omnipotent, foundational fantasy. It is as an account of the fantasy's inauguration and to some degree its overcoming.

Klein is not the only psychoanalyst to refer to Augustine. Lacan also does so. 'The signs of the lasting damage this negative libido causes can be read in the face of a small child torn by the pangs of jealousy, where St Augustine recognized original evil.'[28] After quoting Augustine Lacan moves swiftly on to Hegel's master/slave dialectic, and the attempted destruction of the other consciousness, or other within, that the dialectic foretells. In another context, Lacan makes it plain that that dialectic is the key to the 'most formidable social hell'[29] of the modern era, which he terms the paranoid 'ego's era'. There is no better term for modernity.

For Lacan the ego's era is built on a destructive objectification of the other, together with a destructive objectification in knowledge. The nature of the destructive objectification involved in the master/slave dialectic is left largely unspecified, although Lacan indicates that it means turning the other into a controllable thing. The need to control is what makes the ego's era paranoid; it results from the subject's belief that the object, the objectified one, is out to get it, but this paranoia originates in the subject's own projected aggressive desires toward the other. None the less its paranoia makes the ego anxious, and its anxiety makes it want to control. The objectification of knowledge is also paranoid; it is knowledge based on a need for control. It is knowledge tied to a 'positivist' world-view in which what is seen, or what can be tested or proved to exist, especially on the basis that it can be seen, is privileged. The objectification of knowledge helps construct a world in which only objects (or discrete entities?) are recognized, and they can only be recognized by subjects. In turn these subjects are affected, if not driven, by the objects they construct, objects whose energetic process of construction will be discussed below. Lacan does not pursue this point. He is more concerned with the objectification of knowledge as such; in this concern, he is at one with Heidegger, to whom Lacan frequently alludes, although Lacan has no interest in the objectification of the 'standing reserve' of nature.

In fact generally when Lacan comes to describing how it is that the 'ego's era' comes into being, he is – apart from one brief article on the city, space and aggression[30] – not interested in the era's social dynamics.[31] To deal with these, a more adequate theory of objectification, amongst other things, is required. By this argument, the desires to poison, fragment and destroy the mother's body constitute the process of objectification. After all, the best way to turn someone or something into an object is to kill it. But there are degrees of objectification. The process of mortification begins with how the other is seen, and supposedly known. Klein's account also ties the objectifying desires to the drive for knowledge. While she does not stress visualization in this connection herself, the fact that Foucault ties objectifying power/knowledge to visual mechanisms of control fits with the theses I am elaborating. In addition, we have seen that turning the other into an object also means fragmenting it (in order partly to know it) or poisoning or in other ways attacking it, as well as making it a controllable thing. A similar point is made by Kristeva, who, in an argument which echoes that of Mary Douglas, makes 'abjection' the foundation of objectification.[32] Abjection is the feeling that one has revolting (including excremental) substances within; objectification comes from the need to exclude these substances by depositing them in the other, which brings the other, as object, into being.

Thus far, it seems, we have an account of a psychical fantasy which tallies with the desires encapsulated in commodities. It is this psychical fantasy I am positing as a foundational psychical fantasy. That is to say, I am positing that the desire for instant gratification, the preference for visual and 'object'-oriented thinking this entails, the desire to be waited upon, the envious desire to imitate the original, the desire to control the mother, and to devour, poison and dismember her, and to obtain knowledge by this process, constitute a foundational psychical fantasy.

It is a fantasy which accords certain attributes to the subject, and dispossesses the other of them as and by the process that makes the other into an object, a surrounds (as Heidegger might say), an absent background against which it is present. It is a fantasy that relies on a divorce between mental design and bodily action to sustain its omnipotent denial. In this fantasy, the subject must also deny its history, in so far as that history reveals its dependence on a maternal origin. There is no 'before' before this very present subject. We have also seen how the subject denies time: how it must do this to sustain its fantasy, by imagining that there is no delay between what it desires and the presence of the desired object.

It remains to see of course how far what I have called a foundational fantasy is in fact foundational, how it connects to its macrocosmic enactment, and how, precisely, it connects to instantly gratifying commodities. If, as I have suggested, psychoanalytic insights are gleaned by looking down a telescope the wrong way, and if the fantasy studied in miniature in individuals also exists on the large-scale, how does that fantasy reside without as well as within? The key here lies in energetics: the energetic affects out of which the fantasy is composed. In this chapter, we have laid the grounds for seeing how the foundational fantasy is a paranoid fantasy about autonomous beginning. Through it the subject postulates itself as such, and severs connections with those around it. This subject believes that its fantasies, and the affects that underpin them are its own affair. We need now, first (Chapter 3), to establish that energetic affects exist apart from any one individual's experience of those affects; second, we need to show how it is that those common energies marshall themselves into homologous patterns at both the individual and socio-historical level. For the foundational fantasy, it should be clear, has a certain pattern; more than this, a particular causality. We return to this in Chapter 4. First let us discuss if energies and affects can be held in common.

Notes

1 The distinction between psychical and material reality is Freud's. It has been criticized by Jean Laplanche and J. B. Pontalis, 'Fantasy and the Origins of Sexuality', in V. Burgin, J. Donald and C. Kaplan (eds.) *Formations of Fantasy* (London and New York: Methuen, 1968), pp. 5–34.

2 See, in particular, the well-known seventh chapter of Sigmund Freud, *The Interpretation of Dreams* [1900] in Sigmund Freud, *The Complete Works of the Standard Edition of the Psychological Works of Sigmund Freud*, 24 vols., ed. and tr. James Strachey *et al.* (London: The Hogarth Press, 1957–66) (hereafter *SE*), vol. 11, pp. 163–75.

3 For the most thorough discussion on Freud's relation to Fechner, see Henri Ellenberger, *The Discovery of the Unconscious: The History and Evolution of Dynamic Psychiatry* (London: Allen Lane, 1970). As with most of my references to Freud this is discussed in more detail in Teresa Brennan, *The Interpretation of the Flesh: Freud and Femininity* (London and New York: Rout-ledge, 1992).

4 For representative illustrations of these and many of the following Kleinian ideas from different periods of Klein's work, see Melanie Klein, 'Early Stages of the Oedipus Complex', *International Journal of Psycho-Analysis*, vol. 11 (1928), pp. 167–80 and Melanie Klein, 'Envy and Gratitude', in *Envy and Gratitude and Other Works, 1946–1963 (Collected Writings*, vol. 3) (London: Hogarth Press and the Institute of Psycho-Analysis, 1975), pp. 176–235.

5 The logic of guilt and persecution goes like this; you attack someone or something or some people; guilt, which is the knowledge that you are responsible starts to rise up; but this rising up of guilt is so unpleasant that you repress it, while remaining dimly aware that the other makes you feel really uncomfortable. And because they make you feel uncomfortable, you attack them again, and so the cycle starts over.

6 The most representative if difficult account of the views summarized in this paragraph is Melanie Klein, 'Notes on some Schizoid Mechanisms', in *Envy and Gratitude and Other Works*, pp.1–25.

7 Klein, 'Envy and Gratitude', pp. 201–2.

8 Freud, 'Female Sexuality', in *SE*, vol. 21, pp. 221–43, p. 236.

9 Freud, *Beyond the Pleasure Principle*, in *SE*, vol. 18.

10 Jacques Lacan, 'Aggressivity in Psychoanalysis' [1948], in *Écrits: A Selection*, tr. Alan Sheridan (London: Tavistock, 1977), pp. 8–29, p. 13.

11 The imitation of the original is an often implicit and sometimes explicit theme in discussions of women and technology, particularly reproductive technology. For the founding collection on this theme, see Michelle Stanworth (ed.), *Reproductive Technologies: Gender, Motherhood, and Medicine* (Cambridge: Polity Press, 1987). For a discussion which bears more closely on the issues discussed here, see Vandana Shiva and Ingunn Moser, *Biopolitics: A Feminist and Ecological Reader on Biotechnology* (London: Zed Books, 1995).

12 Jean Baudrillard, *Simulacres et Simulation* (Paris: Galilée, 1981) and Jean Baudrillard, *America*, tr. Chris Turner (London and New York: Verso, 1986).

13 Jean Baudrillard also identifies the loss of the sense of history in America as a fact, not a theoretical lapse.

14 The denial of will also holds for people of different racial and ethnic origin, in terms of a 'belief structure rooted in a concept of black (or brown or red) antiwill, the antithetical embodiment of pure will. We live in a society where the closest equivalent of nobility is the display of unremittingly controlled willfulness. To be perceived as unremittingly without will is to be imbued with an almost lethal trait.' Patricia Williams, *The Alchemy of Race and Rights* (Cambridge, MA: Harvard University Press, 1991), p. 219.

15 Conceptual ties such as this are fascinating pointers to the notion that Benjamin's 'prelapserian state', in which the expressive value of a word was tied to the signifier, may have something to it.

16 A qualification. While omnipotence is tied to the act of hallucination, most non-Western cultures do not regard a hallucination as necessarily deceptive. What is likely in these cultures to be dubbed hallucinatory could as well be styled a vision, or spirit-possession. It is only in the psychoanalytic vision that hallucination is tied in its origin to infancy. I have followed this vision, but its cultural specificity, and the phenomenology it presupposes, is questioned in the book's conclusion.

17 Although Borch-Jacobsen comes close when he pinpoints the core of megalomania in many of the dreams Freud analysed. Mikkel Borch-Jacobsen, *The Freudian Subject* (London: Macmillan,

1989). Borch-Jacobsen's analysis of why narcissism is necessary, in fact the key to, the constitution of the subject is the outstanding discussion of this theme. Also important are Laplanche and Pontalis, 'Fantasy and the Origins of Sexuality', and Jean Laplanche, *Vie et mort en psychanalyse*, tr. J. Mehlman (Paris: Flammarion, 1970), and in *Life and Death in Psychoanalysis* (Baltimore: Johns Hopkins University Press, 1976).

18 Hannah Arendt, *Life of the Mind* (New York: Harcourt, Brace, Jovanovich, 1978), p. 3. It is exactly this *superbia* which is lacking in what Arendt termed 'the banality of evil'. The evil of totalitarianism is banal because it lacks depth. As well as lacking pride, it lacks the other all-too-human motivations for evil: envy, or the 'powerful hatred wickedness feels for sheer goodness' or covetousness, or even weakness. The idea that banality of evil, exemplified in Eichmann, is manifestly shallow is entirely consistent with thoughtlessness, and the bureaucratic manner in which totalitarianism makes human life in its plurality superfluous.

19 St Augustine, *De Civitate Dei* (*The City of God*), Book XIX 12.

20 Ibid., Book XIV 28.

21 Ibid., Books XVI and XIX, and see Julia Kristeva, *Strangers to Ourselves* (New York Columbia University Press, 1991). Specifically, Kristeva refers to Paul's cosmopolitanism, in which foreigners are regarded as equal to other Christians (pp. 79–80) and Thomas More's *Utopia* which she describes as being extremely democratic, 'almost communist': the inhabitants of this utopia tend naturally towards Christianity as an equalitarian philosophy (pp. 116–17).

22 S. Aureli Augustini, *Confessionum* [c. 400], ed. P. Knoll (Leipzig: Verlag von B. G. Tcubner, 1898), pp. 38–9.

23 Peter Brown, *Augustine of Hippo: A Biography* (Berkeley: University of California Press, 1967), p. 327.

24 St Augustine, *De Civ. Dei*, Book XV 5.

25 Ibid.

26 The idea that 'only the best are capable' of *superbia* is understandable enough in the light of the logic of *The Human Condition*. Arendt tells us that 'aristocrat' derives from the verb *aristeuein*, roughly: constantly proving oneself 'to be the best'. Hannah Arendt, *The Human Condition* (Chicago: University of Chicago Press, 1958), p.19. In turn, the wish to be the best is what is lost for Arendt with the loss of the public striving, the *vita activa*, that goes into decline with the rise of the social.

27 Although Augustine uses paternal language minimally, and there was some sense in which he and his colleagues disregarded

traditional gender distinctions. One friend writes to him that he longs to draw milk from Augustine's breasts. St Augustine, *Letters*, tr. Sister Wilfrid Parsons (New York: Fathers of the Church, 1953, pp. 213–14).

28 Jacques Lacan, 'Some Reflections on the Ego', *International Journal of Psycho-analysis*, no. 34 (1953), pp. 11–17, p. 16. Lacan does not give a reference for the quotation from St Augustine. It comes from the *Confessions*. See above, note 22. The observation that Lacan also quotes (in French) reads: '*vidi ego et expertus sum zelantem parvulum: nondum loquebatur et intuebatur pallidus amaro aspectu conlactaneum suum.*' S. Aureli Augustini, *Confessionum*, p. 8.

29 Lacan, 'The Mirror Stage' [1949] in *Écrits: A Selection*, pp. 1–7, p. 7.

30 Lacan, 'Aggressivity in Psychoanalysis', pp. 8–29.

31 But there are allusions to the ego's era throughout his work: allusions that, if they are systematized, make up a theory of the historical trajectory of the ego's era, a trajectory which is very similar to that detailed by Adorno. See Teresa Brennan, *History after Lacan* (London and New York: Routledge, 1993), where I have argued that what Lacan needs is a theory of energy, of the interactive economy, and, of course, of economics. That is what I have outlined here.

32 Julia Kristeva, *Powers of Horror: An Essay on Abjection* [1980], tr. Leon S. Roudiez (New York: Columbia University Press, 1982), pp. 17–32; Mary Douglas, *Purity and Danger: An Analysis of Concepts of Pollution and Taboo* (New York: Praeger, 1966). Douglas's cross-cultural enquiry lends further weight to the notion that what we are dealing with here is a foundational fantasy with a very wide application in some of its aspects.

3

ENERGETICS

My thesis in this chapter is that all beings, all entities in and of the natural world, all forces, whether naturally or artificially forged, are connected energetically. I am calling this an interactive energetic economy. The notion of an interactive economy will help explain how affects and desires can be communicated from the one to the other, and how both the one and the other can be born into affects that pre-exist them.

Now the notion that there is a conative, energetic force coursing through and activating individual subjects and their living environment is not new. It was with us before, and is appearing now. In its naturalistic form, it enjoyed a certain popularity in the guise of pantheism, Romanticism and *Naturphilosophie*. It attained some intellectual respectability in Spinoza's name. Basically, from the seventeenth century onwards the idea comes into disrepute (with Mesmer's manipulative use of it) although there are certain respected exceptions. Thus Walter Benjamin writes:

> They alone shall possess the earth who live from the powers of the cosmos. . . . The exclusive emphasis on an optical connection to the universe, to which astronomy very quickly led, contained a portent of what was to come. The ancients' intercourse with the cosmos had been very different: the ecstatic trance . . . It is the dangerous error of modern man to regard this experience as unimportant and unavoidable, and to

41

consign it to the individual as the poetic experience of starry nights. It is not; its hour strikes again and again, and then neither nations nor generations can escape it, as was made terribly clear by the last war . . . Human multitudes, gases, electrical forces were hurled into the open country, high-frequency currents coursed through the landscape, new constellations rose in the sky, aerial space and ocean depths thundered with propellers, and everywhere sacrificial shafts were dug in Mother Earth. This immense wooing of the cosmos was enacted for the first time on a planetary scale, that is, in the spirit of technology. But because the lust for profit sought satisfaction through it, technology betrayed man and turned the bridal bed into a bloodbath. The mastery of nature, so the imperialists teach, is the purpose of all technology . . . [But] technology is not the mastery of nature but of the relation between nature and man . . . In technology a *physis* is being organized through which mankind's contact with the cosmos takes a new and different form from that which it had in nations and families. One need recall only the velocities by virtue of which mankind in now preparing to embark on incalculable journeys into the interior of time.[1]

Benjamin wrote the above passage in 1925–6, a year before Martin Heidegger published the treatise that was to become *Being and Time*. Like Heidegger, he thinks about the relation between technology and the mastery of nature, and between physics and metaphysics. Yet Benjamin ties technological mastery to capitalism and imperialism. He is also politically optimistic about the possible outcome of this energetic unleashing, seeing it as the source of the proletarian revolts that followed and accompanied the First World War.

None the less, the energetic 'cosmic power' that runs beyond and through individuals is by Benjamin's account at least a two-edged sword. Tied to technological mastery, it is destructive. It can also unleash energy for the good. The idea of connecting forces as two-edged will be fundamental

in what follows. So will the idea that energy can be unleashed; this points to why the notion that humans are closed
or contained entities is now under suspicion, in popular
culture, and under a little nervous scrutiny in the academy.
It points to it because it suggests that the historically shaped
technological shifts have energetic effects on human
beings. This means a new slant on the notion of 'cosmic
connection', one which introduces the dynamics of social
and historical construction as forces which shape energies.
For the main part, this social and historical understanding
of energetic connection is missing in the cosmic consciousness theories that inform the New Age culture,
and which spill over into deep ecology and some of the
theories of the German Greens.[2] While the idea of a
connecting force survives, in New Age culture especially, it
survives on miserable arguments, and is always assumed to
be good.

As I have indicated, the notion of energetic connection
between beings and their environment also survives in popular culture, where notions of energetic connections between
beings are seen as both beneficient and malign. The idea has
returned in a series of blockbuster films ('May the force be
with you') and in writers ranging from Arthur C. Clarke to
Toni Morrison. Morrison's *Beloved* was revolutionary,
ahead of academic time, in writing of psychical feelings and
forces which were not self-contained but crossed between
individuals.

A little investigation suggests that the notion opposed to
psychical energetic connection, the notion of psychical containment, may be historically and culturally specific to the
modern West. Michèle le Doeuff has argued that the late
Renaissance introduces a

> philosophical revolution which gives to the 'I' a
> discretionary omnipotence over the concrete self . . .
> In the Avicennean tradition *my* imagination is not
> really *my* imagination, because it is moved and affected
> by images which I receive, by the other's charm, by
> his or her wishes, beliefs and fears.[3]

Le Doeuff goes on to argue that this tradition is replaced by one which seals the subject off from the influences of others. She suggests that, for instance, Hobbes and Shakespeare 'agree in what they deny: that fancy can pass from one person to another. Each individual becomes a closed space in relation to their fantasmagoria: their desires and dreams are their business'.[4] Certainly we find notions of psychical connections and energetic transmission in Montaigne, whose sixteenth-century essay on the imagination begins with the information that the author is 'one of those who are very much affected by the imagination. Everyone feels its impact, and some are knocked over by it'.[5] Montaigne makes it clear that the imagination works energetically between beings, for better or worse, in sickness and in health. He records how an ill, rich old man asked a physician for advice on how he could be cured. The physician replied that it would be by infecting Montaigne with a wish for the old man's company.

> Then if he were to fix his gaze on the freshness of my complexion, and his thoughts on the youthful gaiety and vigour with which I overflowed, and if he were to feast his senses on my flourishing state of health, his own condition might well improve. What he forgot to say was that mine might at the same time deteriorate.[6]

This idea, that the depletion of the one may enhance the energy of the other, resonates with the theory I advanced in relation to Freud and femininity,[7] but more of that in a moment. It also resonates with Elias's argument that Western premoderns did not have 'an invisible wall' dividing them from one another.[8] But let us step outside the West, for if we put the above gestures together with the cross-cultural argument of Strathern,[9] there is more support for the idea that the 'ego's era', as a Western event, coincides with the advent of the contained individual. Strathern argues that the notion of indivisibility, which underpins the etymology of the word 'individual', is culturally specific, and that other cultures conceive of people as potentially divisible (unbounded or uncontained). Moreover, these other cultures also eschew subject/object thought, to the extent that the subject/object distinction implies a split between mind and body. There are many example of this, but consider La Fontaine's, who shows that not all cultures 'distinguish clearly the material and immaterial (including the social) attributes of persons'. The real unions may lie not between individuals, but between, say, their hearts and livers, which may act in concert.[10]

The idea of the individual as contained is also foreign in the pre-socratic times before the metaphysical stance, and subject/object thought, is born. This period is also (very broadly) one where there is 'no unified concept of what we call "soul" or "personality"'.[11] Using the example of Agamemnon's apology to Achilles, in which Agamemnon claims that he only behaved badly because the gods made him do it, Dodds connects the idea that there is no unified personality with the belief in psychic intervention, by which the gods planted *monitions* (notions, energetic gifts or depletions) in humans which made them act in ways which they felt came to them from without, and for which they could disclaim responsibility whilst retaining credibility.

All this is meant to change with Plato,[12] in so far as Plato inaugurates a subject/object thought: that is to say, in so far as he inaugurates thought in which a distinct and unified subject, as opposed to the dispersed but connected soul of Homer, relates to the world as a separate and manipulable 'object.' In fact, just how 'subject/object' thought arose in the first place is not clear, nor can it be clear until we have established the origin of the foundational fantasy writ large, within cultures. But the point here is that, while subject/object thinking (and possibly the notion of containment) have been with us since the Ancients, these ideas have hardened. I suspect that for a millennium at least, two modes of thinking and experiencing oneself co-existed in the West. The first was the mode of Agamemnon, in which ideas and energies were experienced as coming from without, or as interconnected (thus too the philosophy of the group mind that we find in the work of the Averroists, notably

Siger of Brabant[13]); the second is the individually self-contained mode, the mode of the interior consciousness (as for instance we find, early, in St Augustine). The hardening, or the dominance, of self-contained thought can be tied to the struggle against usury. In the same time period, as the church was struggling to contain usury, the understanding of sin as an event independent of the sinner's intentions began to shift. Initially confessors' manuals focused upon the appropriate penance for the act. But by the early thirteenth century, a sinner's *intentions* determined the gravity of their sin: 'a whole new frontier, introspection, had been created and would slowly transform ways of thinking and behaving. These were the beginnings of psychological modernity.'[14] Asked about whether a man can be contrite if he cannot weep tears, because he has no eyes, 'Caesarius replies, "contrition does not consist in tears but in the emotion of the heart, whose outward signs are indeed tears of the eyes, but the heart has tears of its own."'[15] This sentiment illustrates the increasing movement of Christian devotion toward the idea of an inner life.

Introspection, the interior consciousness, had taken hold firmly by the seventeenth century. My argument that it goes together with object-oriented thought also has tacit support from Charles Taylor whose remarkable synthesis shows how interiority or inwardness, a condition of being an 'individual' with an 'inside', is born and gathers strength with the rise of modernity. 'Thought and feeling – the psychological – are now confined to minds . . . As long as the order of things embodies an ontic logos, then ideas and valuations are also seen as located in the world, and not just in subjects.'[16] The idea of the hardening of the subject/object distinction is also supported in Rorty's analysis of how the mind, as the 'inner arena' of ideas, the 'inner Eye'[17] is born in Descartes' context. For Rorty, this inner arena remakes the distinction between subject and world. This self is also aware of distance, in a way that premodern people were not; this modern self no longer thinks of itself as connected with the cosmos, but as dislocated.[18] Susan Bordo, also discussing Descartes, ties 'the flight to thinking in subject/

object terms' to shifts in the attitudes to mind and body, women and nature.[19] But as Susan James has argued, Descartes, in particular, is not guilty of any 'clear division between mind and body', because he makes a distinction 'between passions and so-called intellectual emotions'. There is a difference between the fantasy that splits mind and body, and the complexities in the thought of Descartes, to whom the philosophy of mind has traditionally attributed that split.[20]

But in sum, there is support for the idea that the force of the subject/object distinction changes over time, as does the notion of individual self-containment. It may be that the idea of the contained individual, who thinks in subject/object terms, based on an 'interiorized consciousness', who is the agent of and responsible for its feelings, fancies and thoughts, is the modern Western exception, rather than the rule. But we still need a theory of energetic connection which enables us to account for changing historical inflections in the experience of it. I will draw on Spinoza in constructing such a theory.

Spinoza is traditionally regarded in the history of ideas as an aberration. At approximately the same time that Descartes was apparently marshalling mind and body into their classic dualistic distinction, Spinoza was developing the view that 'mind' and 'body' (Spinoza's own terms are 'thought' and 'extension') are the equivalent of twin attributes of One Substance. This One Substance is *Deus sive Natura* (God or Nature), an energetic force that is mindful, as well as material, and connects being to being, entity to entity, source to force. The shorthand way of understanding Spinoza is to see him as a pantheist, and despite considerable theological debate, I do not see much wrong with this. What is more interesting is the fact that from the perspective I have outlined, Spinoza is less of an aberration than he is a continuation of the idea of connection. As we have seen, the notion of energetic connection between beings seemed to be the rule rather than the exception in premodern times. A second point of interest concerns the fact that while Spinoza contributed to the Romantic movement in philosophy (after the sixteenth-century all connected thinking came to be designated Romantic and/or irrational), Spinoza himself stressed logic as the greatest good. God is logic, and logic is connection.

Spinoza's key concept here is that of *conatus*: a striving, a logical striving, which took the individual closer to God through action and knowledge. The opposition to the active force of *conatus* is the imagination. The former is a striving for expansion, which Hampshire compares with Freud's concept of the libido, the precursor of the life drive. Ideas of the passive imagination are associated by proximity, rather than the striving logical process which marks real thought, a striving which at its highest would lead to an identity with Nature.[21] For Spinoza the imagination is passive and narcissistic, although of course Spinoza did not use psychoanalytic terminology. But Spinoza's idea of 'imagination' is narcissistic for, because of it, individuals focus inwardly on themselves and their desires, rather than their outward striving. It is through this striving, and the knowledge they attain, that people find their freedom and their connection with God-as-Nature.

In contemporary writing, the idea that there are energetic connections between beings and environment has two main exponents in the academy: Deleuze and Guattari. Deleuze, especially, also expressly connects himself to Spinoza, and more or less to Spinoza's ideas of *conatus*, or striving, *potentia* or power, and the indivisibility of thought and matter, as well as the idea that all things are energetically connected.[22] Like Spinoza, Deleuze and Guattari do not conceive of these connections in terms that are historically modulated. I will come back to this; first, the distinctiveness of Deleuze's theory warrants attention. The difference between Spinoza and Deleuze is that Deleuze wants to replace Spinoza's emphasis on the logic of God-as-Nature, as the One Substance which is thoughtful as well as substantial, with a dice-throwing, desiring chaos which has no logic. Logic, for Deleuze and Guattari, is inseparable from a subject/object distinction (in language and in perception), in which the subject has a rule of signification and related forms of oppression imposed on it, which it in turn imposes on an object. Both logic and the subject/object distinction are inseparable from a bound, contained subject. My disagreement with this position is not the equation of containment with a particular subject/object distinction, but the further equation of both with logic, and the assimilation of all subject/object distinctions under the same structural rubric. One can have an inherent order of connection which is not linear; this is the order found in nature's logic which perpetuates the living: a logic of multitudinous paths that intersect, which works through living things rather than imposing itself upon them from outside and above.

The equation of logic with an oppressive subject/object distinction is based on a common confusion between any order of connection as such and an imposed and limiting rule. While oppressive political regimes exploit the confusion mercilessly in appeals for law and order, order is not the same as imposed rule. That aside: the great merit of Deleuze and Guattari is to have put the Spinozan world-view on the post-structuralist agenda, and with it consideration of a mindful connected physicalism.[23] Their major disadvantage, apart from their treatment of logic, is that they make it impossible to think historically whilst using the framework they advocate. History is styled a metanarrative, and histories which try to account for change partake of a totalizing imposition (etc.). Deleuze and Guattari's rejections of history and of logic also go together: history as a metanarrative is, like logic, an illusory emanation from the subject. But this means that the state advocated by Deleuze – a state of being without or before a subject/object distinction, a state of panting, pulsing flows connecting bodies ungoverned by the rigid law of Oedipus, in a world of discontinuous energetic throws of dice, where subjects are not contained and therefore not subject – it means this state is in some way the natural state. Historically, the best Deleuze and Guattari can do is to argue that capitalism reinforces that state, through its trend to fragmentation. Their brilliant insight about subjective containment as an illusion is constrained by the inability to account for the production of that illusion; by the above brief survey, subject containment has not been uniform in its strength, nor necessarily always with us.

Spinoza's concept of logic makes it possible to think historically, but only because the historical process can be contrasted with the order of logic. By noting the contrast, we come closer to a theory of how it is that the sense of self-containment is historically produced, and how it has hardened historically in the West: a hardening that is becoming global. For Spinoza, logic as the process of connection is the same as the process of connection in nature. Spinoza gives us an account of logic which is not transcendental, not the province of the masterful subject, and not split from the body, any more than mind is split from the body. God-as-nature is One Substance with dual attributes, thought and extension, which cannot be separated although they have to be separately conceived. Because Spinoza sees logic as existing independently of and prior to the human subject, because he does not split thought and matter, Spinoza's philosophy is in fact not guilty of most of the charges levelled against 'the metaphysical systems of the transcendental subject of reason' (supply your favourite reference). He expressly dispossesses the subject of exclusive claims to the logos in a magnificent dispossession which Freud, who acknowledged his indebtedness to 'the great philosopher', could well have added to his list of the great blows against man's narcissism.[24] The three blows to man's narcissism were: (1) the discovery that the earth was not the centre of the universe; (2) Darwin's theory of the descent of species; (3) the discovery of the unconscious, which showed that the idea of conscious control of one's actions was an illusion. Spinoza showed us that man does not have a monopoly on logic.

It should be plain now that Spinoza holds a very different position on logic than do the key thinkers of the post-structuralist canon (Deleuze, Derrida, Foucault and the more nuanced Kristeva), and the advocates of anti-foundationalism. Anti-foundationalism is against 'foundations', defined not in the architectural sense as some analytic philosophers have assumed, but as the assumption that the human being 'founds' his or her own meaning, truth and certainty. Logic is part of the same foundations; it comes from the subject. Derrida especially develops the tie between foundationalism and processes of exclusion; subject-centred criteria for truth invariably exclude some people; and I add they invariably exclude the non-human world. Derrida stresses that to exclude is always to take possession, and thus links logic and truth to the narcissism of the 'self-identified subject', whose narcissism requires that he take possession of, and lay claim to truth, while excluding others from the right to any such claim.[25]

By my account logic exists regardless of, and without special attention to, any particular subject, no matter how present. Yet even though Spinoza's idea of logic is extremely radical, in that it is not subject-centred, it has been neglected in the critique of foundationalism. This critique has not pushed beyond its antithetical position to speculate about an origin before the foundation it takes apart for the narcissistic charade it is. I do not want to do away with Spinoza's radical non-subjective logic in favour of a desiring dicey chaos. In the following chapters, it should be plain that my difference from Spinoza is that I believe that the foundational fantasy (encompassing what Spinoza terms the 'imagination') has been very successful in challenging the original logic of nature. It has constructed its own fantasmatic, technological world, which now actively rivals the original logic, and constructs an alternative to it.[26] By the same argument, we will be able to see how technological shifts have energetic effects on us, and this might help explain why we theorize energy and boundaries in different ways at different times.

If, as I am arguing, the sense of internal containment is historically inflected, then it is inevitable that our theories of energy are similarly affected. Our ideas about energy, our own psychical boundaries, reflect, or to use a more accurate term, literally embody the specific energetic continuums we inhabit.

It remains to see how the foundational fantasy works energetically, and how the sense of self-containment is physically constructed. In examining this, we will also see that the energetic economy following on from foundational thinking (and in turn giving rise to and reinforcing it) is based in inertia. This inertia, which is evidently constructed rather than given, enables us humans to think of ourselves as separate. At the same time, this construction bends living natural energies to its will, in a way that necessarily depletes them, and slows them down. After this, we will be able to see how the inertia constructed by money and the dead world of commodities both induces and reinforces the foundational fantasy within, and how the desires generated in this way feed the fantasy without.

Notes

1 Walter Benjamin, 'One Way Street' [1925–6], in *One Way Street and Other Writings* (London: New Left Books, 1979), pp. 103–4. (Other writings in this volume were published between 1916 and 1937.)

2 Rudolph Bahro, *From Red to Green* (London: Verso, 1984), and Petra Kelly, *Fighting for Hope*, tr. Marianne Howarth (Boston: South End Press, 1984).

3 Michèle le Doeuff, *Vénus et Adonis suivi de gènese d'une catastrophe* (Paris: Alidades, 1986).

4 Ibid., p. 86.

5 M. de Montaigne, in *Essays* [1580], tr. J. M. Cohen (Harmondsworth: Penguin, 1958), p. 36.

6 Ibid., p. 37.

7 Brennan, *The Interpretation of the Flesh: Freud and Femininity*.

8 Norbert Elias, *The Civilizing Process* [1939], tr. Edmund Jephcott (Oxford: Basil Blackwell, 1982), p. 249.

9 Strathern's originality here is to have formulated a systematic critique of the concept of the individual, and to have elaborated on it. Marilyn Strathern, *The Gender of the Gift: Problems with Women and Problems with Society in Melanesia* (Manchester: Manchester University Press, 1988). The concept of the self-contained individual, terminated by death, has been put in question by Maurice Bloch, 'Death and the Concept of Person' in S. Cederroth, C. Corlin and J. Lindström (eds.), *On the Meaning of Death: Essays on Mortuary Rituals and Eschatological Beliefs* (Uppsala: Almqvist and Wiksell International, 1988), pp. 11–22, who focuses on the idea that in some cultures parts of the

body survive after death, and remain in a meaningful unity with the same parts in other (living) bodies. See also the classic Louis Dumont, *Homo Hierarchicus* [1966] (London: Paladin, 1970), on the absence of a concept of individuals in 'holistic' societies.

10 La Fontaine's study is also a critique of Read, for an 'ethnocentric' treatment of the Gahuku-Gama subject/object distinction. J. La Fontaine, 'Person and Individual: Some Anthropological Reflections', in M. Carrithers, S. Collins and S. Lukes (eds.), *The Category of the Person: Anthropology, Philosophy, History* (Cambridge: Cambridge University Press, 1985), p. 130. But Kenneth E. Read, 'Morality and the Concept of the Person among the Gahuku-Gama' [peoples of Highland New Guinea], *Oceania*, vol. 25, No. 4 (1955), pp. 233–82, is also interesting on this question. Read argues that different constituent parts of human personality are considered to reside in different parts of the body and bodily excretions, and that injury to certain parts of the body leads to that aspect of the personality also being injured. Read, 'Morality' p. 265. *See also* D. Battaglia (ed.), *Rhetorics of Self-Making* (Berkeley: University of California Press, 1997) and B. Morris, *Anthropology of the Self: The Individual in Cultural Perspective* (London: Pluto Press, 1994). I am indebted in this research to Sarah Green.

11 Eric R. Dodds, *The Greeks and the Irrational* (Berkeley: University of California Press, 1951), p. 15.

12 A great deal has been accomplished in the name of a firm divide between the pre- and post-Socratics. The pre-Socratics for Heidegger had it all; the post-Socratics lost it. Lacan attributes the distinction between form and matter to Plato. Irigaray has also followed Heidegger in seeing the pre-Socratics as the paradisaical thinkers, from whom Plato and his successors fell into a world where matter and form were split, and the subject reigned over the world without regard for its Being. For the classicist scholar, the idea of an abrupt division is simply not accurate. Martha Craven Nussbaum, *The Fragility of Goodness: Luck and Ethics in Greek Tragedy and Philosophy* (Cambridge: Cambridge University Press, 1986), has traced the pre-Socratic lineage in Aristotle's thought, and argued that it would be a mistake to take the Platonic system as one which ruled out all or most pre-Socratic ideas.

13 Averroes and his followers, like Siger of Brabant, were targets for St Thomas Aquinas, who argued against their concept of a group mind by the *reductio ad absurdum*. They were caricatured in a most unsaintly manner. St Thomas disposed of him with questions such as: 'Do we all have the same ideas simultaneously?'

14 Le Goff, *Your Money*, p. 12.

15 Ibid., p. 91.

16 Charles Taylor, *Sources of the Self: The Making of the Modern Identity* (Cambridge: Cambridge University Press, 1989); and cf. Stephen Jay Greenblatt, *Renaissance Self-Fashioning: From More to Shakespeare* (Chicago: University of Chicago Press, 1980).

17 Richard Rorty, *Philosophy and the Mirror of Nature* (Princeton: Princeton University Press, 1979), p. 62.

18 Keith Thomas, *Man and the Natural World: Changing Attitudes in England 1500–1800* (London: Allen Lane, 1983).

19 Cf. Carolyn Merchant, *The Death of Nature: Women, Ecology and the Scientific Revolution* (San Francisco: Harper and Row, 1980).

20 Susan James, *Passion and Action: The Emotions in Seventeenth Century Philosophy* (Oxford: Clarendon Press, 1997), p. 2, p. 17. Bordo and Merchant confuse both the subject/object split, and the related mind/body split, as products of the foundational fantasy increasing over time, with the history of Western philosophy as such.

21 Stuart Hampshire, *Spinoza* (Harmondsworth: Penguin, 1951).

22 Cf. G. Howie, 'Capitalism and Schizophrenia: A Critique of "The Anti-Oedipus"' (Cambridge University, unpublished Ph.D. thesis, 1992), and Ronald Bogue, *Deleuze and Guattari* (London and New York: Routledge, 1989), on Deleuze and Guattari's intellectual lineage.

23 The affinity between Spinoza and Deleuze is undernoted; there is a tendency to write as if the idea of 'a new materialism' began with Deleuze alone.

24 Yovel quotes Freud writing to an old Spinozist, who called Freud to account for not acknowledging his similarities with Spinoza: 'I readily admit my dependence on Spinoza's doctrine.' Yeshudi Yovel, *Spinoza and Other Heretics* (Princeton: Princeton University Press, 1989), p. 139.

25 Jacques Derrida, *Writing and Difference* [1967], tr. Alan Bass (Chicago: University of Chicago Press, 1978), p. 419; Jacques Derrida, *La carte postale: de Socrate à Freud et au-delà* (Paris: Flammarion, 1980), p. 212.

26 The struggle between the two worlds introduces the historical contrast and sense of change that is absent in Spinoza, an absence reflected (for instance) in his belief that all forms of government that might exist have already been tried.

4

INERTIA

My intention in this chapter is to sketch out a model of constructed inertia. By this, I mean a process whereby energy in human bodies is constrained by a kind of overlay, a rigid map of pathways that parallels nothing so much as the overlay of bitumen roads that binds the earth. Technically, inertia is a relative concept. But as we will see in what follows, Newtonian inertia and what I term 'constructed inertia' are not the same thing. The foundational fantasy constructs 'inertia' in the psyche, and this inertia makes us slower and, over time, old and tired. The construction of commodities and the means to build them has related effects on the macrocosm. These effects are related because, in both cases, pre-existing, naturally given energies are bound into 'fixed points'. By understanding these fixed points we will be able to see, or begin to see, how the psychical experience of the foundational fantasy, and its historical, macrocosmic enactment are linked. They are linked by the manner that fixed points, in turn, construct the sense of time together with the perception of self-containment (which makes it *appear* that the fantasy is an individual affair). In later chapters, we will trace how constructed inertia plays itself out economically, binding energy in fixed forms which cannot reproduce themselves, in an exact parallel with the psychical process. As we will see in Chapter 9, after exploring time and energy in economics, the parallel is more that. But first, we need to consider how a similar process works psychically.

Time is something I theorized at length (and slowly) in an argument that hallucination was the key stone in a psychical constructed inertia, the first fixed point that enabled the subject to experience itself as contained.[1] I now want to recapitulate elements of that theory, both in order to show how it holds for the environment, as well as the psyche, and to expand on the temporal factor in the foundational fantasy.

So far, we have the subject (counterposed to an object) founded by the act of hallucination. What prompts the hallucination is the desire that the longed-for object be present here and now. Yet if we examine Freud's account of hallucination, we find that hallucination not only introduces instant gratification (in theory); in practice, it also introduces delay, and through it, and the experience of waiting, the sense of time passing. In this connection, delay is not really the opposite of instant gratification. It is its alter ego. In Freud's terms, the secondary process comes into being through an inhibition [*Hemmung*] of the primary process.[2] In the primary process, almost all things are possible; it is governed by the pleasure principle, and marked by hallucinatory wish fulfilment, a lack of contradiction, the mechanisms of condensation and displacement, and timelessness, amongst other things. The secondary process is governed by the reality principle. It is the locus of rational thought, directed motility and planned action or agency. When it inhibits the primary process, it checks out or 'reality-tests' whether the image before it is a real perception or an imagined hallucination. In other words, it makes the psyche pause before it responds to the image it is offered. So, on the one hand, hallucination inaugurates a delay; on the other hand, I think that hallucination is a response to a delay, on the grounds that the wished-for instant gratification must be prompted by the experience of a gap between the perception of a need and its fulfilment.[3]

The nature of the primary process is one of the most taken-for-granted yet confused areas of Freud's theory. In addition to the characteristics already noted, the primary process consists of freely mobile energy, and there are reasons for thinking Freud identified it with the 'movement of life' as such.[4] At the same time, *the primary process consists of the pathways in which energy is bound in familiar patterns*, a bondage which leads to repetition, and repetition, in turn, is the hallmark of the death drive. The bound and repetitive pathways of the primary process come into being via repression. They do this because repression is the way the subject copes with the fact that hallucinations do not satisfy the needs that prompt them. The subject has to banish the hallucination, in order to respond more appropriately to the need, and avoid not only the unpleasure of the continuing need, but the unpleasure of the excitations amassed with the hallucination.

But this banishment does not dispose of the hallucination; like all banishments, it only puts the hallucination in another place, which is why Freud writes of its repression. The hallucination stays, and in its repressed form does double duty. It is the foundation of the subject's memory for Freud; and, as I have argued, at the same time as it founds the subject's memory, it founds the unconscious. The subject-to-be has to remember that the hallucination was ineffective, and to use its excitations more productively. 'Memory is evidently one of the powers which determine and direct [an excitation's] pathway'.[5] Memory is also one of the powers influencing judgement, which the ego employs in the delay during which it decides whether a hallucination was real or imagined.

But this memory and that judgement are built on the retention of a lie, of a foundational fantasy that evades subsequent exposure: this is the fantasy that the subject controls the breast, the source of all bounty, that the buck starts here. The repression of the hallucination brings the repressed unconscious into being, together not only with memory but, as we shall see in a moment, direction from a subject-centred standpoint. Indeed this memory and that direction require an unconscious. What we regard as properly unconscious is conscious in psychotics.[6] And psychotic symptoms include conscious hallucinations, absence of memory, or the experience of past events as present, and of course confusion over 'subject-centredness', location and direction, especially the location and direction of ideas, energy, images: these are often conceived as coming from without rather than within, as rays, probes and pronouncements, rather than thoughts and impulses. In turn, this experience signifies a confusion over boundaries. So the repressed hallucination must contribute in some way to the success of the boundaries, the sense of self-containment the subject enjoys.[7]

None of this makes real sense unless it is located in an economy of energy. Freud is insistent that the repression of a hallucination requires a persistent expenditure of energy. But aside from theories of sexual repression,[8] Freud's belief that psychical energy was the key to and means of unravelling psychical knots has received little attention. We need to give it that attention, both for the sake of understanding the interactive/energetic economy that connects being to being, and for theorizing how the subject-centred standpoint, and the self-contained subject, are born. Both depend on the repressed hallucination, as this constitutes a fixed point from which the nascent subject garners its bearings. But uncovering this fixed point means dealing with a level of repression that comes before sexuality and sexual repression.[9]

The act of repressing a hallucination is basic to establishing a sense of space–time in that it establishes a fixed point of reference from which the nascent ego can get its bearings. Literally, its spatio-temporal bearings. This means that the sense of perspective is a construction, as may be the sense of passing time. The idea that the sense of perspective is a construction is attested to by, for example, the fact that when sight is recovered after blindness, the sense of perspective (distance and size) does not necessarily accord with the perception of others. It is often completely out of proportion with what we know as reality. The idea that the sense of passing time is also constructed is demanded by the theory that space–time is a continuum; time is measured in terms of space, and the interval between one event and another depends on the speed it takes to cover the distance between them, and speed, in turn, depends on the potential motion or energy of the body involved.[10] But if one looks more closely at what the initial repression of hallucination involves (the process by which the hallucination becomes unconscious), it is evident that something is happening to energy in the process, and also that 'time' is measured relative to something other than the constructed space–time of which it is also part.

I suggested that a hallucination is prompted by the delay between the perception of a need and its fulfilment, and noted that Freud (although he does not postulate an initial delay) argues that the secondary process comes into being through an inhibition of the primary process, which in turn amounts to a further delay. Postulating an initial delay between the perception of a need and its fulfilment as the condition of hallucination means postulating a prior state in which perception and need coincide, or in which the delay between the need and its fulfilment was shorter. The fact that there is an intra-uterine state which is experienced before birth meets the requirements for this prior state. That is to say, if we suppose that, *in utero*, there is no experience of a delay between perception and need, or that any delay is shorter, the intra-uterine state should constitute another pole against which the construction of space–time could be measured. It is a pole of more rapid motion.

This supposition will have more substance if one considers what happens to psychical energy when it is bound. Freud's argument on this[11] has led to a debate amongst psycho-analysts as to whether the bound pathways that come into being through distinguishing between hallucination and real perception are on the side of the life or the death drive. The key opposed positions here, which I shall only sketch briefly, are represented by Laplanche and Lacan respectively.

Laplanche disputes Lacan's location of the ego on the side of the death drive.[12] He does so on the basis of an interpretation of Freud's assumptions about inertia. (For Laplanche, these were 'outdated even at the close of the nineteenth century'; from my investigation, they were not outdated. Freud invented an idea of inertia which had some justification precisely in nineteenth-century interpretations of Newton's first and second laws, not before.) The essence of Laplanche's argument is that, first, the ego is a kind of giant fantasy in itself. This much he has in common with Lacan. Laplanche bases his view of the ego as a fantasy in itself on the *Project*, where Freud posits the ego as a mass of cathected neurone pathways. Or, if we put this in terms of Freud's subsequent, less physiological vocabulary, the ego is a mass of pathways in which psychical energy is bound.

Laplanche also argues that Freud confused the principle of inertia with the principle of constancy. The former is a state in which there is no motion, nothing. It is the desire to restore an earlier state of things in which the governing principle is rest. In Freud's 1920 formulation on the death drive, he termed it the Nirvana principle.[13] The principle of constancy is the desire to keep energy constant. For Freud, freely mobile energy will follow the path of least resistance, which is the path towards Nirvana. For Laplanche, while the ego is a giant fantasy, it is none the less a vital one, in that its bound pathways are the essential means for action against or towards what is necessary for sustaining life. There is no essential contradiction between its actions towards or away from life and the principle of constancy. These ideas will be plainer if we return to the contrast between energetic connection and self-containment. This is paralleled by Freud's contrast between freely mobile energy on the one hand, and bound energy on the other. By my argument, freely mobile energy is the energy of nature, the *Deus sive Natura*, and bound energy is that of self-containment. Bound energy is also the product of the binding of nature in the fixed points of commodities 'outside' the psyche. But, in the first instance, let us consider what happens to psychical energy when it is bound.

Bound energy is the product of experience. When you deal with something once, you set up a 'neurone pathway' for dealing with the same thing again. This pathway depends on the binding of energy, so that, in one way, bound energy saves time. In another way, the very binding of energy means that a person is more inclined to repeat a pattern for dealing with a situation, even after the situation has changed. This is because energy will flow along the paths that are familiar to it, and these paths might be completely inappropriate for dealing with a novel situation. The repression that brings both the pathways and the ego into being figures here; bound energy flows along pathways that are unconscious. In addition, there are two complications which reinforce the notion that the bound is on the side of the deathly. The first is that the ego is less likely to adapt and follow new pathways in a situation which arouses anxiety. Furthermore, it is precisely the protracted attachment to any fantasy (which must necessitate a bound pathway) that characterizes neurosis. Such attachments make it harder to act upon the world; they are similar in their effects to anxiety, in that they counter 'the movement of life'.[14] The movement of life here is equivalent to freely-mobile energy, in turn, the same as the life drive. By the same logic, the attachment to the bound pathways resonates with Freud's controversial concept of the death drive. What is bound, by my argument, is more likely to be on the side of the death drive, Freud's 'Nirvana principle', precisely because the bound pathways, the fixed points, impede the movement of life. Too many of them increase anxiety, neuroses and psychical rigidity in general. They leave one less lively, with less energy, over time. At the same time, one needs some of those bound pathways in order to survive.

Now it would be easy enough to take a liberal approach here, and say that, on the one hand, the ego and bound pathways are necessary: one has to deal with life's exigencies. This is the position of Laplanche. On the other, if too much psychical energy is bound, if the pathways are too rigid, if anxiety is greater, then vaulting ambition overleaps itself and the result is deathly. This is the position of Lacan. Both positions appear reasonable. But adopting this reasonable solution means overlooking the more radical implications of Freud's theory of inertia. To that theory we now turn.

For Freud an inert state is a restful one, and any body seeking rest will seek to be inert or motionless. In supposing this, Freud to an extent invents an idea of inertia, in that he equates a common-sense understanding of the term with its meaning for physics. In physics, inertia does not mean lack of motion. It is the tendency to restore the state of motion existing before a disturbance in equilibrium. But Freud's interpretation is a potentially productive mistake.

The fact that a hallucination has to stay repressed involves a persistent expenditure of energy. It means that freely mobile energy is permanently bound in the repression. The repression of the first hallucination thus constitutes a fixed point in relation to freely mobile energy, and we can call this fixed point and the bound pathways which spring from it 'constructed inertia'. In other words, Freud, by my argument, was theorizing how inertia is constructed relative to the freely mobile energy in which the subject-to-be is conceived. The fixed point of the repressed hallucination founds the subject as a potentially discrete entity in psycho-energetic terms, not only because it founds its memory, not only because it is the point of reference for future decisions about true and false, real and imagined, but because it founds an energetic system which gives the subject boundaries: an ego or a self-contained identity. A few more words are in order to make this plainer.

As the state *in utero* could well be one of more rapid motion (freely mobile energy is not impeded in calling or responding), this living state could be restful in that it appears to be without the conflict contingent on delay, and therefore 'timeless'. In other words, what leads freely mobile energy on its quest for the path of least resistance is not the notion of constructed inertia as Freud understood it, but the memory of a state of timeless (yet, relative to the subsequent sense of time, more rapid) motion. It is interesting therefore to note that the experience of 'no time', of a sense of 'time suspended' has been recorded in writings by mystics: those dedicated to subordinating the ego, as the impediment standing between themselves and God. This experience of no time is interesting because by this analysis the ego is composed of fixed points and pathways that are founded in delay and the first awareness of time passing. But this would also mean that the existence of a timeless universe extends beyond the mother's womb, that there is a 'faster' timelessness which can be regained without regression.[15] But this is the mystic case.

In general the spatio-temporal notion of rapidity only comes into being after the fact: that is to say after birth, and the experience of delay. The point is that after the fact, the resultant slow plight of the ego is measured retroactively, in spatio-temporal terms, against the prior intra-uterine state. In addition, the very thing that leads freely mobile energy into conflict with the exigencies of life is the fact that it encounters a point of resistance. If there was no resistance, nothing would ordain that energy to follow paths set up from the subject's standpoint and there is no *a priori* reason why freely mobile energy could not regain its prior rapid motion. Naturally, this means external as well as internal points of resistance, for it would be a travesty of what logic underlies Freud's reasoning on the ego to reduce the points of resistance the ego encounters to its own self-sustaining fantasies. The ego evidently encounters other points of resistance that would harm its chances of living (very bad weather, aggressive others, etc.), and to these it has to respond. None the less, as the pathways for coping with these exigencies multiply, and as, or if, they become the only pathways we follow in relation to life's exigencies, we become more rigid. This is one reason why, I think, we age, aside from animal biology. There are too many familiar pathways restricting freely mobile energy.[16]

What I want to suggest now is that the pathways which direct energy make the quest for Nirvana deathly. In other words, the subject-centred pathways are the problem, not the nature of the energy which flows through them. On the other hand, without this energy, there would be no movement towards a deathly end. There is no energy outside the freely mobile energy of the life drive. The differentiation between the life and death drives lies not in the energy they in fact share, but in the pathways anchored in fixed points formed through repression. What makes the death drive deathly is the fact that the subject seeks to regain its prior state on the basis of the same pathways which fix its subjectivity in place. In other words, the only way it can regain the prior state is to do away with the pathways, but on these its subjectivity depends. In one sense, then, the idea that life tends towards death is based on a mistake about direction.

But let us keep to the point. If there is no resistance, there are no bound pathways, hence no death drive, but there is also no subject. This is because, without a fixed point, there is nothing that appears to mark the subject out as separate, with an individual history and a personal memory. A poor thing, but its own. But the fact that the subject has to expend energy in maintaining this repressed fixed point and the pathways that follow from it leads to a further paradox, which by my argument can only be resolved in terms of an intersubjective economy of energy. In fact this economy is already implicit in the idea that in the state *in utero* there is no delay between the perception of a need and the response to it. To suppose that there is no delay is to suppose that there is a system of fleshly communication between two parties; it is the maternal organism that responds to embryonic messages.[17] This both establishes and embodies what I term the original logic of the flesh, a system of connection and communication that may contribute to the generative grammar of language.

In this fleshly logic there is no separation between thought and substance: the message and the response are communicated in biochemical codes which are meaningful precisely because they are interactive: they involve two parties. Another name for this fleshly logic is found in Freud, who writes of a 'common source' [*gemeinsame Quelle*] at base of language and affect alike.[18]

After birth, an intersubjective economy makes itself felt in terms of energetic *attention*, and in the transmission of affects and emotions from one party to another. This transmission is presupposed by Kleinians and Lacanians alike in the clinic; and, more recently, by Laplanche. For Lacan, the child is always the symptom of the parents, meaning it carries the unconscious desires of the other. This desire, transmitted in infancy, actually gets into the child, but the energetic implications of this idea are untheorized. Laplanche goes further, arguing that the unconscious in the child is actually created by parental deposits, but how these deposits are made is energetically obscure. Similarly, Kleinians work with the idea that the 'feelings' the analyst has are actually a communication from the analysand about the analysand's feelings; yet how they are transmitted from one party to another is not discussed. This lack of discussion is surprising, as the notion of migrating affects questions the subject already 'in question' in a most radical way. It questions something that has been unchallenged. Structuralism and post-structuralism have argued for the construction and deconstruction of the subject at linguistic and social levels, while the idea that our 'feelings' are socialized has a much longer-standing theoretical currency. But the idea that these feelings are none the less 'ours' (even if they are socialized), and not someone else's, is retained.

Despite a lack of curiosity about the mechanism of transmission, the Kleinian corpus does include a theory claiming that one person can contain the emotions of another, and in some way give the other unconscious as well as conscious attention. It does not say how, but it says that it is done. The theory is Wilfred Bion's.[19] Bion argues that the mother's containment of the projected aggressive, sadistic impulses of the infant is the condition of the infant's learning to think. He also argues that the attention the mother gives the infant is a condition of its thinking; by attention, Bion evidently means something stronger than interest. The mother more or less lends her intelligence, and this loan is evidently capable of crossing from one apparently discrete body to another, which suggests it has to have a material existence itself. The material or physical existence of energetic attention is the cornerstone of my theory of an intersubjective economy of energy. It is the means for resolving the paradox of how it is that the subject keeps going while it simultaneously resists, meaning expends energy on itself. The attention or attentive energy received from another means that the subject-to-be is able to deal with a problem that would be difficult for it to resolve if it existed in a self-contained energetic system.

65

But this facilitating attention is not perceived for what it is. In part, this is because attention comes hand in hand with the desire of the other, with the image the other gives (I term the conjunction of attention and image an imprint). In larger part, it is because the infant confuses the imprint of the other with its own hallucination. The two form an interlock, which is one boundary or border for constructed identity.[20] As the infant has no means for formally differentiating itself from the other, it has no means for differentiating the restrictive fixity of hallucination and image from the facilitating attention that comes with the latter. It can imagine that it is the source of the attention it receives, just as it imagines it is or controls the breast. Indeed, this very imagining could be occasioned by the lack of differentiation, and would explain the *ressentiment* that is always a part of envy: the sense that the thing envied has been unfairly removed, that it really belongs to oneself. And the subject-to-be most surely resents the fixity it needs, but fears, as it struggles into a new world of space, time, language and the existence of other people.

In the next chapter, we trace the path of proliferating commodities, showing how energy is bound in them in the same way that freely mobile energy is bound in the repression of a hallucination. On this basis we will be able to see how the ego's era tries to make itself total, or global, and how it reinforces the psychical power of the foundational fantasy in the process. But, as I tried to show in the preceding chapter, in theory at least, the idea of the subject as a contained entity is being re-examined, and we need to see why this is so. This is a matter I return to in the book's conclusion, where I will suggest that we are dealing with something like a three-stage process: first, a period before, or 'another place' where the idea that human beings are contained (and therefore subjects) is not axiomatic; second, the era of the contained subject, which coincides with the ego's era; and third, the present period in the West, where containment is breaking down in a hallucinatory culture. But this three-stage idea is only suggestive; as I noted at the beginning of Part I, the history of the concept of the contained subject is one which would require far more detailed investigation. That investigation is the condition of working out how specific genealogies intersect with the totalizing trend we confront in capital's acting out of the foundational fantasy. In the remainder of this book, what I try to do for the most part is outline a general theory of one side of the history of this acting out, otherwise known as the history of the ego's era: the totalizing side. Accordingly, I concentrate on the manner in which the production of commodities for exchange acts out the fantasy and makes totalization an actuality.

To sum up the argument of Part I: on the basis of a hypothesis about an intra-uterine state, and an intersubjective economy of energy, I have argued that hallucination makes us self-contained because it divorces mindful agency from the matter that executes it – matter it makes passive in fantasy – *and* because hallucination situates the subject in a fixed place, from which it functions at a slower pace, in energetic terms. These points are related. We think in terms of thought divorced from matter because the divorce sustains the omnipotent illusion at base of a subject-centred standpoint. Yet the hallucination is not immaterial in its effects, however fantasmatic it is. It does, through its repression, effect a divorce between freely mobile and fixed energy, and this division functions henceforth as a seal which closes the subject off from the knowledge and experience of its interconnection. It gives it a boundary; this boundary also cements the imagined separation of thought and energetic substance, precisely because it does effect the beginnings of a material split between them. Energetic substance is manifest in anything from motion to the intermediate experience of affects: affects are especially important as a category in which some of the original indissolubility of thought and substance are retained; they keep the tie to matter, as emotions are indubitably corporeal, at the same time as they reflect ideational responses; we can regard them as the slower-motion residues of the original connection between thought and substance.[21]

Yet while the subject's fixity does in fact make it distinct relative to a state of more rapid and interconnected motion, fixity can only make the subject distinct, after birth, if the state of more rapid motion is not confined to the womb. This means there has to be a field of contrast which has the same effects and the same benefits as the flesh, but which is lived in after birth. The obvious candidate for this field of contrast is the unbound primary process, the life drive, but what is that, other than nature? To nature overall I have attributed the same process of connection and inherent logic, the same inseparability of thought and substance experienced *in utero*. This attribution will make more sense if we note that the split between mind and matter, as it has been described here, is also the split between the individual and the environment. This has to be so by the implications of this argument so far. We can only be self-contained in relation to an environment with which we are potentially connected. The boundary the subject erects is a boundary against freely mobile energy and excitations in general. The contrast with the intrauterine state explains the omnipotent aim of the pathways that redirect the life drive on the basis of fixed points, but the experience of the intrauterine contrast is not the end of the experience of more rapid motion.[22]

In the next chapter, I will suppose that the construction of a commodity binds energy in the same way that it is bound in the repression of a hallucination. The energy bound in commodities is that of living nature; it correlates with Freud's 'freely mobile energy'. I have suggested that the paths of freely mobile energy and those of the life drive are the same, as freely mobile energy follows the path of least resistance. Freely mobile energy only follows this path because something exists that resists. Like the hallucination, the commodity provides a point of resistance, in that it encapsulates living nature in forms which are removed from the flow of life. It functions analogously with hallucinations in that it makes living substances inert relative to the energetic movement of life. We can assume that the more of these relatively inert points there are, the slower the movement of life becomes. It is the idea of this 'slower movement' which is the key to the exhausting nature of modernity.[23] As we will see in what follows, this slow movement underpins a different sense of time, one that appears faster, but is in fact slower, than that of life.

The idea that nature also provides a more rapid energetic field of contrast will have more substance when we see how the technological production of commodities plays out the same dynamics, in relation to nature, as the foundational fantasy does in relation to the maternal body. In other words, the relation between commodities and nature enacts the same dynamics of fixity, inertia and the abolition of time, dynamics which require the diversion of the energy of the Life drive. Evidently, this means the Life drive not only works between people in an intersubjective economy, but between nature, including people, and technology, in what for convenience I have called an interactive economy. The reader will recall that this term is used to stress that energetic connection is not only naturalistic; energetic connections are forged by technologies as well. This was Benjamin's point. The importance of this idea is that it counters the uncritical holism that characterizes thinking about 'cosmic connection'. We can be historically constructed, we can construct history, but these actions have physical effects on the energetic economy we inhabit.[24] In turn, these effects rebound on us.

The idea of the interactive economy means that, in the microcosm of the psyche, the effects of the foundational fantasy are felt more strongly as the fantasy is acted out technologically. Thus, for instance, Klein's belief that the infant wants to poison the mother with its excrements, to cut her up and fragment her, becomes more plausible. It becomes more plausible because the infant psyche, as yet unbound, becomes a catch-all through which historically constructed energies flow. Amongst these are impulses directed towards poisoning and cutting up nature. In the contained psyche, the psyche that retroactively claims the impulses it experiences as its own, the impulse to poison and fragment is expressed on a smaller scale. It is expressed in terms of the tiny concepts to hand, where 'poisons' are something expelled by the body, and the world is the mother.

Who is to say which came first here? The impulses as they are recorded in the psychoanalytic case study, or as they are manifest on the larger scale? The mindset or fantasy predates its technological enactment, but it was socially enacted in more limited ways long before this present. Still, the psychoanalytic discovery, in these times, of the ingredients of the fantasy in each and all suggests the impulses are stronger. We will come back to the question of priority in Chapter 9. Priority, after all, presupposes that the psychical fantasy exists independently of its material version, and that one or the other came first. Priority presupposes a sense of causality and symmetrical time, although this, in the end, may be the most illusory yet material bequest of the foundational fantasy.

Notes

1 Brennan, *The Interpretation of the Flesh: Freud and Femininity*. Basically, apart from the discussion of the life drive, and the death drive as a matter of direction, which are new, the next section summarizes that argument, so I have not given extensive references to Freud; the interested reader can find them there.
2 Freud, *The Interpretation of Dreams*, p. 601.
3 Of course this has consequences for real perception as well as imagined hallucination. One cannot respond immediately to the former. It has to be evaluated. Nothing visual can be taken for granted. What is more, it only becomes taken for granted at the price of establishing familiar pathways for psychical energy to follow. The second is that, as we will see, Lacan ties anxiety to spatial constriction. The argument on bound and freely mobile energy is one that Freud attributes to Breuer, and Breuer attributes to Freud. Sigmund Freud and Joseph Breuer, *Studies on Hysteria* [1895], in *SE*, vol. 2, p. 194.
4 See Chapter Ten below and Teresa Brennan, 'Essence Against Identity' in *Metaphilosophy* Vol. 27 Nos 1 & 2 Jan–April 1996, pp. 92-103, and in *Is Feminist Philosophy Philosophy?* (ed.) Emma Bianchi (Evanston, IL: Northwestern University Press, 1999), pp. 73–85.
5 Sigmund Freud, 'Project for a Scientific Psychology' (*'Entwurf einer psychologie'*) [1895], in *SE*, vol. 1, p. 300.
6 Jacques Lacan, *Le Séminaire, livre III: les psychoses* [1955–6] (Paris: Seuil, 1981), pp. 1ff.

7 I suspect that sound is critical in constructing these boundaries, and giving the subject its distinctive 'self'. Freud talks of how the superego begins through internalizing the parents' voice-residues, and perhaps this should be taken literally. This would mean that the subject's boundary is a spatio-temporal construction which is also based in some sense on soundings.

8 For instance, Herbert Marcuse, *Eros and Civilisation: A Philosophical Inquiry into Freud* [1956] (London: Routledge and Kegan Paul, 1987).

9 Freud terms the force that represses hallucinations primal repression, which he distinguished from repression proper, or secondary repression. Sexuality is tied to repression proper. This repression is connected to primal repression (of some idea or ideational event), in that this establishes a nucleus which attracts subsequent 'proper repressions' towards it.

10 There are several excellent histories of physics and the story of the shift from one dominant paradigm to another, but see in particular Jennifer Trusted, *Physics and Metaphysics: Theories of Space and Time* (London and New York: Routledge, 1991). For reasons of space, I cannot give an exposition of the relevant paradigm shifts here.

11 Freud, 'Project for a Scientific Psychology'.

12 Laplanche, *Vie et mort en psychanalyse*.

13 Freud, *Beyond the Pleasure Principle*, p. 56. Freud's argument on bound energy is elaborated in his 'Project for a Scientific Psychology'.

14 Freud, *Inhibitions, Symptoms and Anxiety* [1926], *SE*, vol. 20, p. 148.

15 Jacques Derrida, Drucilla Cornell, Teresa Brennan, 'Discussion' in Emma Bianchi (ed.) *Is Feminist Philosophy Philosophy?*.

16 Teresa Brennan, 'Social Pressure', *American Imago* (September 1997), pp. 210–34.

17 It means that the mother is not, as Aristotle had it, a passive garden in which a tiny, active, fully formed homunculus is planted, and grows of its own accord. Aristotle, *The Generation of Animals* [*c.* 335 BCE], trs. P. H. Wicksteed and F. M. Cornford (London and Cambridge, MA: Heinemann, 1934). The tendency to regard the mother's role in gestation as passive persists past the discovery of ovulation. It is evidently, however, only the assumption that the mother's role is passive if things go right. That the mother's body can actively upset the development of the embryo is acknowledged and stressed when things go wrong. Thus the injunctions not to smoke, drink and so on during pregnancy are an oblique recognition of the mother's agency.

Needless to say, I am not arguing for feckless pregnancies, merely for an extension of the logic that underlies strictures against them to a recognition of a positive agency, which just might lead to some interesting biological research. Kristeva has also argued that the fact of maternity and existence *in utero* influences all later psychical development. She has done so partly on the basis that there is no effective division between mother and embryo, and that their merging abolishes a subject/object distinction. See Kristeva, 'Stabat Mater' in *Tales of Love* Leon Roudiez (trans.), (New York: Columbia University Press, 1987) pp. 234–63. Irigaray makes a similar point about the placenta, see *je, tu, nous: Toward a Culture of Difference* Alison Martin (trans.), (London: Routledge, 1993) pp. 37–44. Irigaray does not comment much on this herself, the implications are drawn out by Kelly Oliver in *Womanizing Nietzsche: Philosophy's Relation to 'The Feminine'* (London: Routledge, 1995) pp. 187–93. I suppose the difference between the argument I am putting, and Oliver's, Irigaray's and Kristeva's is in fact a difference of degree, and a difference in elaborating the premise and following through on its consequences. To say that pregnancy reveals a state where there is no subject/object distinction is to point to a remarkable fact. But what do we do with this fact? How is the subject/object distinction abolished? I have argued that it is abolished by a rapidity of communication which is only possible where this rapidity is not impeded by the fixed points at base of subjectivity, which leads us into the various implications for nature and technology, as well as the psyche, discussed in the text.

18 Freud was not speculating on the intra-uterine state, but on the connection between hysterical symptoms and the words they reflect. Thus 'a stab in the heart' referred to an affective response located originally in the heart, a location recalled in words. The implication of this for Freud is that language and affect are originally one, but become split.

19 Wilfred R. Bion, *Learning from Experience* (London: Heinemann Medical Books, 1962).

20 The second border is provided by the constitution of sexual difference. See Brennan, *The Interpretation of the Flesh: Freud and Femininity*.

21 Originally I used the word 'feelings' for the 'slower motion' residues of the mixture of thought and matter. Subsequent to writing this I have argued that the term 'feelings' should be reserved for the 'finer feelings' involved in the discernment of the other's affects (a question I do not treat in this book), and

kept the word 'affects' for the projective emotions, such as aggression. 'The Faculty of Discernment' (unpublished paper).

22 The experience of energetic connection after birth is discussed in relation to Freud's concept of excitations and a 'protective shield' against them in Brennan, *The Interpretation of the Flesh: Freud and Femininity*.

23 This idea is also developed in my 'Social Pressure'.

24 By this, I mean not just that we interfere with the biosphere. We may also be creating physical energetic effects which function on the broad scale like 'feelings', mixtures of natural and technological forms of energy, atmospheres that feel like hell.

Part II

ECONOMY

This book began with the idea that Mammon rivals God as nature. Having outlined the psychical dimensions of this rivalry, and the way it works at a microcosmic level, I turn now to its economic mechanism: the creation of an artificial as distinct from a natural time. This artificial time is based on money and commodification. Time, as a glance through the various chapter headings of *Capital*[1] makes plain,[2] occupied Marx as well as the 'bourgeois economists'. But the temporal dimension in Marx's value-theory has been downplayed, obscured by Marx's own emphasis on subjective human labour-power as the key factor in profit. In what follows I will try to use Marx's value-theory without this subjective emphasis. I will argue that, used this way, it becomes a theory of time and speed, a theory which explains inertia in terms of the binding of nature in the fixed points of commodities and reveals how the devil's parody works. Money reproduces itself as if it were a living thing, creating a hell on earth which simultaneously does away with the nature it rivals. Just as the foundational fantasy appropriates the creativity it envies while it tries to destroy it, so money appropriates nature's creativity, and does destroy. Read without its subjective emphasis, Marx's value-theory shows that profit depends on the fixed points of commodities proliferating at nature's expense.

But why the labour theory of value? It is the least used and possibly the most criticized aspect of Marx's *oeuvre*, yet it remains unique in its stress on the 'two-fold' nature of a commodity.[3] In a market system, a commodity is always produced for exchange, and has exchange-value. But it also and always has use-value, and there can be no use-value without nature, or natural substance. Because of Marx's emphasis on the two-fold nature of a commodity, the labour theory of value can become a theory whose essential contradiction is between natural energy and the time or speed of exchange. Marx, however, saw this basic contradiction in terms of labour-power and technology, where labour-power alone adds value, but where value will necessarily be diminished, as more is spent on technology. Technology adds no value in itself, but more has to be spent on it, in order for capital to produce in the fastest time possible, and thus compete. Understanding of this contradiction has been limited because of Marx's subject-centred perspective which singled out labour for special treatment: labour was the subject, nature was relegated to the realm of object.[4] Marx is explicit. Labour is the 'subjective factor', the 'subject'. Nature and technology are the 'objective factor', the 'object'. The 'subjective factor', labour, is living energy. In the last analysis this is how Marx defines it. By contrast to the 'livingness' of labour, nature and technology alike are assumed to be dead. For Marx, living labour, the subjective energetic factor, is meant to be the sole means for realizing surplus value. Other natural forces are assumed to be as dead as technology, and in their deadness assumed to add no surplus value. More than this: labour realizes surplus value because it is a variable factor. Marx calls it 'variable capital', whereas nature and technology are supposed to be constant, constant in that they add nothing. They are 'constant capital'. But if nature or certain natural forces are shown to have an energetic property in common with labour-power, the 'essential contradiction' has more explanatory power. Nature is the source of all value, and ultimately of all energy, but the inherent dynamic of capital is to diminish this value and this energy in favour of time and technology. This argument is set out in Chapters 6 and 7 especially. Up to p. 86 of the next chapter (Chapter 5) is expository. Those confident of the labour-theory of value and of Marx's use of the subject/

object distinction could move towards its last sections rapidly.

Overall, Part II's chapters suggest how Marx's value-theory would work without his subject/object distinction. They do so with very broad brush strokes: these chapters follow a speculative path, whereby the conclusions I reach are entailed by the internal logic of the narrative. There are many overlaps between my speculations and existing writings on Marx. But I could not have reached the conclusions I do through the standard route of exposition and critique (and it would be artificial to pretend I had). The advantage of this speculative logic is that it results in an argument which, if it is right, has implications not only for the environment, but for how the approach to many standard problems in Marxist thought might be reformulated. Moreover, while David Harvey and Fredric Jameson[5] in particular have focused on how space replaces time in modernity, no-one has identified the (labour) theory of value as the explanatory key to this replacement.

Notes

1   Most of this discussion is based on *Capital*, given that this is the text where Marx's political economy is presented in its most developed form. However, I also draw extensively on the *Grundrisse*, and refer to Marx's other writings. I have referred to the main works cited by name: *Capital*, and the *Grundrisse*.

2   In addition to the temporal dimension which is integral to the labour-theory of value advanced in volume 1 of *Capital* (see the next section), Marx's interest in time is reflected in volume 2 of *Capital*, where we find headings such as 'The time of circulation' (V), 'The time of purchase and sale' (VI/1), 'The turnover time and the number of turnovers' (VII), 'The time of production' (XIII), 'The time of circulation' (XIV), 'Effect of the time of turnover on the magnitude of advanced capital' (XV). Volume 2 is sub-titled 'The process of circulation of capital'. It is generally regarded as the least interesting of the three volumes of *Capital*, and this may be because 'time' was so much the preoccupation of the bourgeois economists Marx was writing against, and of mainstream economists since. Marxists assume that time is important, or appears to be important, only at the level of the

fantasmatic or 'mystical' appearance of capital's movements. Marx distinguished between this fantasmatic level and the level of real exploitation of surplus-value. The distinction between these levels is of particular importance in the following argument, precisely because the fantasmatic level is material in its effects, as Marx was the first to acknowledge in writing on the fetishism of commodities. But in the light of the 'reality' of the fantasmatic, time once more comes into its own.

3   Amongst other things, sympathetic critiques focus on the neglect of supply and demand, gender and the environment. The 1970s' generation of feminists tried (and failed) to deploy Marxist political economy in analysing patriarchy. We have yet to see the results of recent attempts to wrestle with the environment from a Marxist standpoint. Roughly speaking, the rich work on the environment that is indebted to Marxism assumes: (a) that Marx had overlooked the finite limitations on nature (which he had); and (b) that capital would exploit nature in order to make a profit (which it does). For a general survey of literature on the environment, see Andrew Dobson, *Green Political Thought: An Introduction* (London and Boston: Unwin Hyman, 1990). For a survey on the literature on Marxism and the environment, see Martin Ryle, *Ecology and Socialism* (London: Radius, 1988). Probably the leading radical non-Marxist exponent of environmental thinking is Murray Bookchin, *The Ecology of Freedom* (Palo Alto: Cheshire Books, 1982). There are excellent articles by Ted Benton, 'Marxism and Natural Limits: An Ecological Critique and Reconstruction', *New Left Review*, vol. 178 (Nov./Dec., 1989), pp. 51–86; and also M. Goldman and J. O'Connor, 'Ideologies of Environmental Crisis: Technology and its Discontents', *Capitalism, Nature, Socialism*, no. 1 (1988), pp. 91–106; and other contributors to the journal *Capitalism, Nature, Socialism*.

4   The odd thing is that with the partial exceptions of Deleuze and Guattari, and Spivak, the attention to the subject/object distinction in general, and binary oppositions in particular, has stopped short of criticizing these oppositions and their effects on Marx. See the discussion of Deleuze in Chapter 3. Spivak analyses the use of oppositions, and the subject-position, in Marx's value-theory, but insists on a 'materialist predication', in express distinction from Deleuze and Guattari. Gayatri Chakravorty Spivak, *In Other Worlds* (New York: Methuen, 1987), pp. 154–5 and *passim*. In another context, Hugh Willmott explicitly queries how thinking in subject/object terms affects understanding of the labour process. Hugh Willmott

'Breaking the Paradigm Mentality' in *Organization Studies* vol. 4, no 5 (1993), pp. 681–719.

5   David Harvey, *The Condition of Postmodernity: An Enquiry into the Origins of Cultural Change* (Cambridge, MA: Blackwell, 1989) and *Justice, Nature and the Geography of Difference* (Cambridge, MA: Blackwell, 1996). Fredric Jameson, *Postmodernism, or the Cultural Logic of Late Capitalism* (Durham: Duke University Press, 1991).

5

THE TIME/ENERGY AXIS

On the opening page of *Capital*, Marx announces that 'A commodity is, in the first place, an object outside us, a thing that by its properties satisfies human wants of some sort or another.'[1] A commodity in short is an object made for a subject. Marx takes this obvious subject-centred definition for granted, and why should he, as a nineteenth century thinker, have not? Yet because he thinks in subject/object terms, Marx excludes natural substances, aside from human labour-power, as sources of surplus-value. I will argue here that he has therefore overlooked that various natural forces are potentially identical to labour-power in their capacity for adding energy.

To begin drawing this argument out I turn first to Marx's analysis of the labour process, for it is here that Marx's basic suppositions about humans and nature, and the division that exists between them, are most evident. In the analysis of the labour process, as in the analysis of a commodity, Marx abstracts from certain circumstances. Here, the abstraction does not take the form of leaving certain factors aside, but of considering the labour process independently of the particular form it assumes under given social conditions (for Marx, whether they are hydraulic, feudal or contemporary does not matter). In the labour process,

> man of his own accord starts, regulates, and controls the material re-actions between himself and Nature. He opposes himself to Nature as one of her own

forces, setting in motion arms and legs, head and hands, the natural forces of his body, in order to appropriate Nature's productions in a form adapted to his own wants.[2]

For our purposes, the important point to stress is that this independent relation between man and nature is one of opposition, wherein nature is the object to be controlled. Marx sees the original subject of labour, the earth, as existing 'independently of man',[3] as did the tools the earth provided. By virtue of this independence, man is subject in any social epoch, whether or not the means of production exist as raw materials and machinery; that is, natural substances which have already been mixed with labour, or as substances directly provided by nature. At the same time, Marx repeatedly acknowledges 'the ever lasting Nature-imposed condition of human existence'.[4] He never loses track of the fact that there is no exchange-value without use-value; use-value always comes first in the subanalyses that make up the text of *Capital*. Yet Marx, like capital, regards the nature-imposed condition of existence as if it were unconditional.

Aside from the problem posed by ground rent,[5] Marx treats nature as an unproblematic variable, aligning it with tools or technology. Nature and technology alike are the object. Jointly they constitute the 'means of production', which Marx defines as the 'objective factors' while he defines the 'subjective factor' as labour-power.[6] As the means of production encompass both tools or technology (which are rarely living) *and* nature (which generally is), this means that things living as well as things dead are defined as objects counterposed to a subject.

In the capitalist mode of production, this counterposition is all the more critical, as the subjective factor, labour-power, is reckoned as the only factor capable of creating surplus-value. Marx is unequivocal.

The same elements of capital which, from the point of view of the labour process, present themselves respectively as the objective and subjective factors, as means of production and labour-power, present themselves, from the point of view of the process of creating surplus-value, as constant and variable capital.[7]

As in every other epoch, under the rule of capital, the subject alone creates value. This universalized subject-centred position, by virtue of a powerful abstraction, has superceded a more fundamental distinction between the living and the dead. Yet as we will see, it is the livingness or energy of labour-power that is critical in its ability to add value, and which seems to make it unique amongst the other commodities entering into production. For labour adds value to the product in two senses. First, labour adds exchange-value to the product because of the difference between labour and labour-power: it is the only subjective factor in the production process. For Marx, the means of production cannot add value to the product precisely because they are objective; there is no subjective variation between the labour-time taken to produce them, and the value they contribute to the finished product. This is the temporal dimension in value addition. Second, labour adds value to the product not only because it contributes more than it costs, but because this value is materialized in the product. More exactly, the materialization of living labour is inseparably tied to the transformation of the product. This is value's energetic dimension. Marx writes expressly that 'Labour-power itself is energy transferred to a human organism by means of nourishing matter'[8] and 'By labour-power or capacity for labour is to be understood the aggregate of those mental and physical capabilities existing in a human being, which he exercises whenever he produces a use-value of any description'.[9] It is quite clear that it is the daily and generational restoration of these capabilities or vital energy[10] that constitute the cost of labour-power, and that labour-power only exists in a 'living vital body'.[11]

As the subject/object distinction subsumes other living substances, aside from labour-power, under the category 'object', we need to ascertain if there is anything in living labour that distinguishes it from these other living entities, substances, forces or sources. We need to ascertain this before we can argue that if the subject/object distinction is dropped, while the emphasis on energy, substance and time is retained, Marx's labour-theory of value retains or regains some of its life. The question of what is living in Marx's theory deserves closer investigation.

Marx's argument for distinguishing 'living' labour from nature applies to all modes of production. It is a tautological argument that does no more than reiterate the subject/object premise on which it is based, but it effects this restatement by equating the subject with the living and the object with the dead. In this argument objectification is a process that stills, fixes and/or ends the life of the other, but this objectifying process is referred to as transformative or life-giving.

The notion that the process is life-giving (when it is not so necessarily) rests on Marx's definition of the objective factors, which makes no distinction between living nature and technology. Marx generally assumes that the raw materials entering into production, whether they exist as natural substances or 'raw materials proper' (that is natural substances which have already been altered by labour in that they have labour mixed in) are liable to dissolution.

> It is living labour which preserves the use-value of the incomplete product of labour by making it the material of further labour. It preserves it, however, i.e. protects it from uselessness and decay, only by working it in a purposeful way, by making it the object of new living labour power.[12]

Or else Marx treats natural forces and sources as he treats the instruments of production in the labour process; he treats them as if they are already dead. 'Living labour must seize upon these things and rouse them from their death sleep, change them from mere possible use-values into real and effective ones'.[13]

While Marx has 'raw materials' in mind here, it is clear

that he does not distinguish between the types of raw materials entering into production (corn, for instance, is one of the objects manipulated by labour in agriculture[14]), as well as the mode of production in which those raw materials figure. In all cases it seems that the energetic act of labour preserves the instruments and the raw materials of production, and thereby preserves the labour (if any) already embodied in them. Moreover, for Marx, labour preserves substances at the same time as it consumes them; these substances are *consumed* in that they lose the material form they had prior to the production process. Marx is very aware that the labour process as he has defined it may be a process of consumption. Its constituents 'are in truth consumed, but consumed with a purpose, as elementary constituents of new use-values, of new products, ever ready as means of subsistence for individual consumption, or as means of production for some new labour process'.[15]

Marx says of a given raw material, in the context of his argument that materials are liable to decay were it not for labour, that 'it becomes extinct in one form of use-value in order to *make way for a higher one, until the object is in being as an object of immediate consumption*'.[16] So here we have the highest use-value defined in terms that are consistent with instant gratification; the more readily consumable, the higher the use-value. Here we have labour producing objects accordingly. Here too we have this transformation of something into a commodity, an object for immediate consumption, presented as an act of preservation.

The difference between labour and nature

But if we focus on the energetic quality capital has brought as a seemingly incidental part of its exchange with the worker, it is plain that this quality at least is not one which is unique to labour. It applies equally to nature. Man

> can work only as Nature does . . . by changing the form of matter. Nay more, in this work of changing the form he is constantly helped by natural forces. We

see, then, that labour is not the only source of material wealth, of use-values produced by labour. As William Petty puts it, labour is its father and the earth its mother.[17]

Nature, too, transforms the form of matter, and transformation, we have shown, is by nature energetic; it is a substantial embodiment of the energy used in transformation. So is there anything that really distinguishes Father Labour from Mother Nature and does so in a way that makes the difference between labour-power and labour the sole source of surplus-value? I noted that other natural substances capable of producing energy have to be *made* to do so. The fact that labour is more or less voluntary might make it unique. Yet under the rule of capital, fewer and fewer are in a position of real control, let alone ownership. It is paradoxical therefore that, apart from the talk of living labour, the only real argument Marx gives us for distinguishing labour and nature concerns the will.

We pre-suppose labour in a form that stamps it as exclusively human. A spider conducts operations that resemble those of a weaver, and a bee puts to shame many an architect [*Baumeister*] in the construction of her cells. But what distinguishes the worst architect from the best of bees is this, that the architect raises his structure in imagination before he erects it in reality. At the end of every labour-process, we get a result that already existed in the imagination of the labourer at its commencement. He not only effects a change of form in the material on which he works, but he also realises a purpose of his own that gives the law to his modus operandi, and to which he must subordinate his will. And this subordination is no mere momentary act. Besides the exertion of the bodily organs, the process demands that, during the whole operation, the workman's [*Arbeiter*] will be steadily in consonance with his purpose. This means close attention. The less he is attracted by the nature of the work, and the mode in which it is carried on, and the less, therefore, he enjoys it as something which gives play to his bodily and mental powers, the more close his attention is forced to be.[18]

To raise the structure in one's imagination, as the architect does, before erecting it in reality, is to be in a privileged position in production, not at all the same as that of the workman. If one really is an architect or master builder, one is probably involved in petty-bourgeois production, where one is both boss and worker simultaneously. Generally, to realize a purpose of one's own in production is to be in a position of ownership or control. Yet although the architect example and one's 'own purpose' are crucial in the discussion of what makes labour 'exclusively human', the positions these presuppose in the division of labour in production, or a mode of production, are not discussed. Marx moves rapidly from the architect's will to the 'workman's will' as if these 'wills' had the same field of play. In fact, only the architect and others in similar positions use their imaginations, and realize their own purposes, although it can be claimed that all who work or labour use their wills. The difference is between a will that realizes one's own purpose, and a will that is the vehicle for subordination to another. But either way, *the exercise of a will is unneccessary for the production of surplus-value.* Again and again, Marx shows how in its attempts to maximize surplus-value extraction, capital will downgrade if not virtually eliminate opportunities for the worker to use the will that is meant to distinguish him or her from 'nature'.

As far as the uniquely human capacity of labour is concerned, the subordinated will is not far from the direction-taking machine. The difference between the machine and the docile, direction-taking worker is that the latter is capable of disputing direction, and of voluntary movement, but whether these are sufficient to make labour the sole source of surplus-value is another question. To the vast extent that capital needs portable direction-takers, to the extent that these cannot be replaced, labour-power and labour are crucial and irreplaceable in the production of surplus-value. But there is in theory nothing inevitable here. If portable direction-taking could be carried out by machines and cyborgs, if the constant capital expenditure in producing them could be kept within limits, surplus-value would still be extracted from other natural forces. The second matter to be noted is that although there are few production processes in which all forms of productive labour are absent, there are some. There are no processes producing commodities with use- and exchange-value that take place without *any* energy derived from natural sources.

In fact, generally, the inability of labour to impose its own will on what will be made makes for serious complications as far as Marx's definition of productive labour is concerned. The only unambiguous definition of productive labour excludes the work of overall design and control,[19] and this raises real empirical problems. For instance, Poulantzas' definition excludes the middle class from the category of productive labour, but the middle class has expanded drastically in size in the heartlands of advanced capital, which raises the question as to the source of the surplus lived off by the middle class, as well as the owning class.[20] It is the service sector[21] (which caters to our instant gratification) of the middle class which has expanded most, and this sector is definitely not productive in the technical sense. If more live off total surplus-value than produce it, or live off it more than they produce it, then there has to be another source of surplus-value. To a degree this is explained by imperialism, although this explanation is not sufficient, as we will see. But the main issue at this point concerns the unique value-producing nature of labour-power.

Marx predicted that when centralization, in the physical form of ever-larger spatial conglomerates, and the monetary form of monopolies accelerated, the worker would be reduced more and more to an adjunct of the machine. This is because increases in the size and speed of the productive forces, the technology and division of labour required to produce more and more commodities within a shorter and shorter space of time, entailed maximizing detail labour.

While so many of Marx's predictions have been wrong, this one has much in it. The separation of control from the energy labour-power is capable of materializing has increased apace, leading to 'the concentration of knowledge and control in a very small portion of the hierarchy'.[22] Energy is less and less directed by the labourers.

In this respect, Marx's theory, especially as his successors developed it, strikes its best-known accord with Weber's account of rationalization. It also draws out, and this remains one of its luminous strengths, the process whereby the majority of human beings are forced into the position of 'objects', lacking the opportunity to exercise intentionality in production. Lukács theorized this process as irrational rationality;[23] for Weber himself, it was instrumental, as distinct from substantive, rationality. Instrumental reason, the efficient regulation of means and ends regardless of human and natural rhythms and needs has been a major theme of Adorno and Horkheimer[24] and other members of the Frankfurt school, who see objectification as weakening the willful resistance to capital.[25] In production, productive labourers have no goals of their own, although Marx notes that human action is always goal-oriented,[26] and goal orientation is the keynote of being a subject.

Under the rule of capital, under the rule of time, if an object is something that lacks mindful will, productive labourers, in so far as they are reduced to an incarnation of energy which they do not themselves direct, become objects. In these ways Marx's value-theory is an account of how the world is more and more a world of objects. It accounts for the solidification of the very distinctions it presupposes: a world of divided subjects and objects, where the aggression and anxiety marking out these positions is reinforced by an economic aggression that is also deadening in its effects. In that divided world human beings, as they become objects lacking the opportunity to express subjectivity, are squeezed into an alignment with nature, which has been treated as a series of discrete or potentially discrete objects all along.[27] In large-scale centralized production, these human and other natural objects are directed by subjects, but subjects they are not. Subjects are dying out. Labour-power precisely does not exercise the thing that makes it distinct: its will.

In analysing the foundational fantasy, I outlined how subjective capacities are appropriated from an other, whose agency is denied. In capital's labour process, subjective capacities are also appropriated; as centralization proceeds, more and more people are positioned as objects. It remains to see how this world of objects is created economically, and how this creation simultaneously replaces time by speed and space.

The origin of profit

In the context of nineteenth-century political economy, it was Marx's great discovery that profit originated in production, not distribution. Profit originated in the difference between what labour added in production within a given time, and the time taken to reproduce labour-power. Marx regarded this distinction between labour, which is what is done at work, and 'labour-power', which is the 'capacity to work', available for sale, as his most important contribution to political economy, his most significant move beyond Ricardo.[28] It was crucial for Marx because it pinpointed the source of profit, or surplus-value. It did so because it recognized that under capital the capacity for labour, as labour-power, could be bought and sold like any other commodity in the free exchange of the market. In all other modes of production, the buying and selling of labour was in some way restricted. A profit is made because what labour adds in production, *during a given time*, is worth more than what it costs to maintain and reproduce labour-power, *at a given time*. This is labour-power's 'socially necessary labour-time'.

In fact socially necessary labour-time sets the value of any commodity, although how far labour-time as such *is* 'socially necessary' is determined by technology. Labour-power working with primitive technology adds no more value than labour-power working with technology that is advanced. Thus labour-time, as a concept, runs technological time and labour together. This is also true of exchange-value, as the exchange-value of a commodity is measured by its abstract labour-time.[29] This exchange-value is 'no substantial thing', Marx insists. It is immaterial. Yet, as we have seen, Marx also says that labour-power, like labour, is always 'energy'.

The relation between time and energy will become plainer if we recall that the means of production include both the inanimate tools or technology used to work on nature, and nature itself. These are the 'instruments' and material for labour: the 'object' otherwise known as 'constant capital', or the 'objective factor' in production. Marx further divided this constant capital into two forms: fixed and circulating capital. Fixed capital was literally embodied in fixtures: buildings, machinery and so on. Circulating capital includes forms of energy and raw materials.[30] Labour is the subjective factor (or 'variable capital') because it can add more or less value.

We need to note two more of Marx's premises. The first is about how capital must, because it is governed by competition, expend more on constant capital in centralized production sites. The second is about the political effects of this centralization. On the first point: to be governed by competition is also, for Marx, to be governed by time. When Marx predicted that more and more wealth would be embodied in constant capital and expenditure on the means of production, he did so because 'our capitalist', or 'moneybags', as Marx also called the agent involved in the profitable enterprise, had to ensure that more and more commodities were produced and put into circulation in a shorter and shorter *space of time*, in order to capture a share of the market. Our capitalist can only do this by expending capital on technologies which produce faster, or at any rate no less rapidly, than other comparable enterprises and by reducing unit production costs. The greater the outlay on constant capital, the more capital-intensive production is, the lower the unit-production costs (in general). They are lower because more fixed capital expenditure per unit output is the means to economies of scale. Our capitalist compensates to some extent for what he loses in real profit (surplus-value contingent on variable capital) by capturing a larger share of the market. But he can only do this if he moves fast.

Precisely because they involve honing the time of production through detail labour,[31] the expanding technologies necessary for economies of scale require centralized production sites, embodied in ever larger spatial conglomerates. Now as I just mentioned, but wish to stress, this is a necessary but not a sufficient condition of successful competition for our capitalist. He can only capture his share of the market by putting his commodities into circulation no less rapidly than his competitors. In order to both produce and distribute as rapidly as or more rapidly than his competitors, he has to acquire the means of production and labour-power within a timescale appropriate to his production and distribution. In Marx's schema, acquisition belongs to the sphere of exchange. Marx himself insisted on the *interdependence* of what he designated the four spheres of capital: production, reproduction, distribution and exchange, but production was always the privileged sphere. Yet once value-theory is read without its subjective emphasis, without the distinction between labour as subject and nature as object, as its emphasis shifts to time, the speed of distribution and exchange becomes cardinal. Distribution and exchange, while they are answerable to speed, obviously involve space and the regulation of space.

But keeping to the exposition. For Marx, the very expenditure on more rapid means of technological production contains the seeds of capital's demise in that constant capital, of itself, can add no surplus-value. The ability to do so remains the property of labour or variable capital alone. Yet because technology is the means by which the production of profit is speeded up, and given that it can offset a fall in profit in the short term, capital will tend towards the situation where it relies more on technology than it does on living labour; thus, to borrow an example from Marx's *Capital*, a machine capable of producing X amount of cloth may require only one labourer to work it, while many labourers would be required to produce the same amount of cloth without the machine. At this point the dual aspects of 'labour-time' stand opposed once again. Labour as energy is the only thing that adds 'more', but unless it adds it within the prevailing socially necessary labour-time, capital will not make a profit.

One cannot begin to grasp the importance of the material, energetic dimension in value-theory without taking account of how natural energy works on and in a continuum of natural substances overall. This is why terms such as 'biosphere' and 'ecology' have their current currency: they embody the recognition that the natural continuum is precisely that; you cannot inflate or diminish one part of it without having effects on another. The notion of the transfer of matter into energy – more exactly, the idea that matter *is* energy – is also part of contemporary currency, and in one sense it belongs in Marx's.

Just as nourishing matter feeds labour-power, so is nourishing matter fed by other natural substances. Just as the reproduction of labour-power cannot take place without or outside the cycles of natural reproduction, neither can the reproduction of other natural sources and forces. So, on the one hand, all these forces and sources are connected. On the other, they are not equal from the temporal perspective of capital. But, for the time being, I will continue to refer to natural sources and forces without qualification, whilst bearing in mind the obvious point that not all of them add energy, or useful energy, to the same extent. Some of them add more energy than others, including labour-power. Some add less.

As we have seen, for Marx himself, energy can only be added by living labour ('the subject'); all other constituents of production are supposedly lifeless ('the object'). As far as the behaviour of capital is concerned, their 'livingness' is irrelevant. But this does not mean that it is irrelevant to the inner workings of production, or to a value-theory that is not subject-centred. It is important to remember that Marx, in discovering what he thought was the source of capitalist profit, also showed how capital loses consciousness of that source; it spends more on constant capital, less on the variable capital that adds value. This source was so obscure that part of it remained hidden even from Marx.

93

The assumption that labour alone is living, and that nature is not, is entirely consistent with the omnipotent foundational fantasy. Marx not only identifies the 'living factor' with subjective human agency; in the characteristic fantasmatic gesture of reversal, he endows the subject alone with the capacity to give life. The gesture is only possible where it is assumed that nature gives nothing of itself; and that is only possible in a mode of production in which living nature is marginalized. Yet it is exactly this marginalization, a concomitant of industrialization, that Marx generalizes to all epochs, regardless of its evident historical specificity. But the gesture of itself is not enough to make labour-power alone the source of value, to the extent that this source is that which lives.

As labour-power is precisely energy, even 'tension',[32] it has everything in common with other natural forces, capable of realizing energy as humans can. For that matter, it has a potential affinity with natural substances which are inanimate as well as animate, in so far as these can be made into sources of energy. Of course they still have to be *made* into these sources, and on the face of it, it would seem that only labour has this power of making. But our immediate concern is with their energetic dimension.

Like labour-power, natural sources and forces are commodities capable of releasing and adding energy. Like labour-power, they have a certain time of natural reproduction, which means that, potentially, the value they add in production can be greater than their reproduction time. Like labour-power, they can add more or less energy in the production process. Of course, we have to distinguish between these natural sources and forces in terms of (a) what kind of and how much energy they generate, and (b) the cost of acquiring them, in relation to one another and to labour-power. Both these points will be addressed at length below.

The point here is that because Marx begins from a subject/object world in which all things, artefacts and natural substances, are already commodities, objects for the consumption of a subject, he may suppose that the only new substantial value added in the (industrial) production process is the *energy* newly materialized by labour in the product.

But once labour-power is treated as a source of energy, one form of all natural sources of energy, once the opposition between subjective and objective factors is replaced by one between living nature and the commodified dead, then value-theory's logic can be extended. We can keep the logic that led Marx to break capital down into two components: constant and variable capital. We can even say that variable capital is the source of surplus-value, while constant capital is not. We can deduce too that the greater the outlay on constant as opposed to variable capital in production, the less the surplus-value extracted. We can deduce further that the imperative to produce more in the shortest possible time will lead to a greater outlay on constant capital.

But the change we will make, on the basis of my argument that, *at the level of substance, productive living labour-power should not be distinguished from other natural sources and forces that materialize energy*, is that we will assume that *all natural sources of energy entering production should be treated as variable capital and sources of surplus-value*, and some can be replaced by others. The logic of this replacement will encompass labour-power. If another natural substance can supply what labour supplies, it too counts as variable capital. Moreover, this series of assumptions entails that *there is no real check on the speed with which variable capital can be used up, apart from whether or not a particular form of variable capital can be replaced*, meaning its reproduction has to be guaranteed.

If all energetic sources entering production add value, the tendency of the rate of profit to fall will be offset.[33] It will only fall where constant capital is really 'fixed' in relation to labour-power, in that no other natural force figures in production, disguised as constant capital. It is readily disguised by Marx's original conceptual armoury. Just as his definition of the 'objective factors' elided nature and technology, so too does the definition of 'circulating capital' elide technological and natural forms of energy. Our redefinition of variable capital encompasses natural sources of energy, which have been conceptually locked up in the concept of circulating capital.

The significance of circulating capital in this epoch is recognized by Marxist political economy; for Mandel, it is probably the most important factor within it, because of its increasing range and speed.[34] My rereading of value-theory will explain this phenomenon as one that is basic rather than incidental: the range and speed of circulation is one key to how surplus-value is extracted and profit made. However, by making speed basic, we will be able to explain capital's behaviour in relation to agricultural commodities: including animals, whose reproduction is speeded up whenever possible. We will even be able to resituate labour-power in a privileged and crucial place in surplus-value extraction, a place that depends on its voluntary portability (which does after all mark it out from other sources of energy). But these things can best be done after a more detailed discussion of the idea that one energy source can be replaced by another in industrial production.

The process by which one energy source will be replaced by another can be formulated in terms of what I call a *law of substitution*. According to this law, capital, all other things being equal, will take the cheapest form of energy adequate to sustaining production of a particular commodity at the prevailing level of competition. Many of these energy forms will be refined; they will be – from one to many times – removed from their natural state. But this does not mean they cease to be valuable. They only cease to be this when their capacity for adding energy is exhausted. Up to this point, their value may be increased as other forms of energy (including labour-power) are mixed into them, although this mixing can also diminish energy sources overall, especially when their reproduction is ignored. It will be discounted whenever possible; forms of energy are likely to be cheaper when reproduction is discounted.

From this standpoint, I can now qualify 'natural sources and forces'. Some substances are more ready forms of energy, or more readily converted to, and add more energy than others. In everyday thinking, the extent of the energy they have or add is precisely what makes them valuable. And this cuts both ways. If labour can stand in for another energy source more cheaply and more effectively, it will be the source chosen. The points are that at the level of substance, the material energetic level, the common denominator is energy, not labour-power, and that all energy sources, including labour-power, vary in what they cost compared to what they add.

Do we have any warrant other than the direction of my argument for assuming that capital will operate by a law of substitution? In fact a similar assumption about substitution was made by Marx, when he discussed the various permutations of labour-power as a commodity. Capital, he claimed, would not hesitate to force down the wage as much as possible (keeping 'socially necessary labour-time' to the minimum) or import (that is, replace) labour-power from another source. This is why Marx assumed that the need to extract surplus-value could lead to the immiseration of the working class. He assumed that as the 'organic composition' (meaning the ratio of subjective variable capital to objective constant capital) of capital changed, and a greater expenditure on constant capital meant less outlay on variable capital, it may be that the only way to make a profit or increase surplus-value was to keep wages down, to the extent that the level of subsistence became the level of near survival. Thus also the advantage to capital of a reserve army of labour (the unemployed and the *lumpenproletariat*), whose existence in itself is a way of keeping the price of labour-power down: it weakens the bargaining power of the working class.

Now if certain natural forces capable of adding value within the sphere of industrial production are interchangeable, then capital's range of cheap options is greatly extended. It has in its back pocket not only Marx's 'reserve army' but Heidegger's 'standing reserve' of nature. In line with the logic of substitution that governs capital's selection of labour-power, where it will always, all other things being equal, take the cheapest option, it should be the case that capital operates by a general law of substitution where living forces overall are concerned. If one energy source can stand in for labour, and stand in more cheaply, it will be the source chosen. Such energy sources, from coal to oil, can offset any trend towards the immiseration of the working class, to the extent that they can stand in for labour.

The effects of the law of substitution here are similar to those wrought by imperialism, and the creation of a labour aristocracy. When Lenin, following Marx and Engels, argued that a labour aristocracy, a richer segment of the working class, could be created through the exploitation of other sections of that class, nationally and internationally, he was drawing attention to how the rate of surplus-value extraction of one portion of the labour market could be less in one place if it were higher elsewhere.[35] We can now see how a similar 'benefit' to portions of the labour-market can be effected through increasing the rate of surplus-value extraction of other natural entities and things. Thus, to pick up on Marx's nineteenth-century cloth example at the beginning of the twenty-first century: natural fabrics cost more than synthetic ones, whose raw materials can be 'repro-duced' at a faster rate, unless the natural raw materials as well as the fabrics are reproduced and produced in 'cost-effective' labour-intensive centres, where the cost of labour-power is so low that the fabrics can compete internationally (*100% Cotton: Made in India*).[36]

In certain circumstances, and from its peculiarly ruthless perspective, capital might be concerned for the repro-duction of natural forces, and the substances on which they depend, but it will only be concerned in so far as these sources (i), if replaced, provide a continual cheaper option and (ii) are irreplaceable. While capital had to be concerned about labour-power's capacity to wage resistance, it only has to be concerned about resistance in relation to natural forces when they are spoken for. Needless to say, natural forces, substances and non-human beings, are un-unionized, unrepresented, and therefore frequently not spoken for. It is ironic that the avant-garde at this point discourages speaking on behalf of the other.[37]

Notes

1 Karl Marx, *Capital*, vol. 1, p. 43.
2 Ibid., p. 173.
3 Ibid., p. 179.
4 Ibid.
5 On Marx and rent in general, see Ben Fine, 'On Marx's Theory of Agricultural Rent', *Economy and Society*, vol. 8, no. 3 (1979), pp. 241–78. Marx treats rent not as a property of the land but of social class relations to the land. In one respect this opens out the possibility of considering land in terms of its direct exploitation, in that differences in fertility lead to different returns to the same capital investment as do differences in location. Marx terms this differential rent; it applies to competition within the agricultural sector. He counterposes differential rent to absolute rent. Absolute rent is the result of competition between the agricultural sector and other sectors in the formation of surplus-value overall. The problems absolute rent poses for the always difficult question of how value is transformed into price are particularly acute, and Marx makes little headway with it in what is perhaps the most poorly revised section of *Capital* (vol. 3, part VI). An analysis of Marx's writings on the question of rent would be an ideal test case for the redefinition of variable capital proposed in Part II.
6 Marx, *Capital*, vol. 1, p. 179. Initially, having abstracted from nature Marx distinguishes three elements in the labour process, but the abstraction enables him to reduce the three elements to two: one subjective, the other objective. In the first place, Marx analyses the labour process by resolving it into its (three) simple elementary factors. There are '(1) the personal activity of man, i.e. work itself, (2) the subject of that work and (3) its instruments' (p. 174). These elements can be isolated in this way because the labour process is *always* 'human action with a view to the production of use-values, *appropriation of natural substances to human requirements* (p. 179, emphasis added). Initially this appropriation of natural substances to human requirements is unmediated. Nature is 'man's larder and his tool house' (p. 175). Yet it is clear that even in discussing unmediated production, Marx assumes not only that the basic elements of the labour process exist independently of social forms; he also assumes a relation between these elements which is independent of social forms. Man is opposed both to the 'subject of work', or nature, and the instruments or tools. Together these become the object, or objective factors, and any tension between tools and nature disappears.

7 Ibid., p. 202.
8 'Nourishing matter' is a standard nineteenth-century term. Ibid., p. 207 *n*1. In *Capital* it also appears in a footnote to Sir John Gordon's 1855 report on the adulteration of bread. Ibid., p. 171 *n*2.
9 Ibid., p. 164.
10 Ibid., p. 169.
11 Ibid., p. 165 (trans. mod.).
12 Marx, *Grundrisse der Kritik der Politischen Ökonomie Europäische* [1857–8] (Berlin: Verlagsanstalt, 1953); *Grundrisse*, tr. M. Nicolaus (London: NLR/Allen Lane/Penguin, 1973), p. 362.
13 Marx's examples in this discussion tend towards natural substances which have already been cut out of the process of natural reproduction, but the difference between natural substances which cannot re-enter natural reproduction and those which can is not discussed. Marx, *Capital*, vol. 1, p. 178.
14 Ibid., p. 177.
15 Ibid., p. 178.
16 Marx, *Grundrisse*, p. 361 (trans. mod., original emphasis).
17 Marx, *Capital*, vol. 1, p. 50.
18 Ibid., vol. 1. The negative connotation of will conjures up the account of labour in the early Marx, particularly the Marx of the *Economic and Philosophical Manuscripts of 1844*. Labour 'is activity as suffering, strength as weakness, begetting as emasculating, the worker's *own* physical and mental energy, his personal life – for what is life but activity? – as an activity which is turned against him, independent of him and not belonging to him'. Karl Marx, *Economic and Philosophic Manuscripts of 1844* [1844], tr. M. Milligan (Moscow: Progress Publishers, 1959), p. 67 (original emphasis). In the early Marx, this negative notion of labour-as-will occurs in the context of the discussion of alienation (see below).
19 Nicos Poulantzas, *Political Power and Social Classes* [1968] (London: New Left Books, 1973).
20 The category of productive labour has been the subject of intense debate. First, if one controls the means of production to any extent, how far one's labour is productive labour will depend on the relation between the value added in production and the wage. If the cost of the wage, the socially necessary labour-time, is commensurate with or more than the value added in production, the labour is not productive. Now of course the more one controls, the larger the wage-share. Indeed, it becomes a salary. Salaries mark the middle class, not the working class of productive labour. The separation between

ownership and control characteristic of monopoly – and late capitalism – becomes widespread, and the class of controllers correspondingly so extensive, that the size of the middle class is expanded. Traditionally, the middle class is divided into two sections: the old petty bourgeoisie (small businesses such as shops and small producers) and the new middle class, the lower stratum of the class who own and control the means of production, who blend into the upper echelons of the working class. These people are technical or supervisory workers, professional groups defined by the fact that they are paid a salary more than the amount of it. It is the new middle class that has grown in size – and this is contrary to the polarization between the working and capitalist classes predicted by Marx. Probably the most systematic attempt to define the new middle class has been that of Poulantzas, *Political Power and Social Classes*, who bases much of his analysis on the distinction between productive and unproductive labour. His strict adherence to the productive labour criteria makes it harder to get into the working class than to get out of it. For Poulantzas, the old and new middle class, or petty bourgeoisie, have in common the charactcristic of vacillation. They are essentially unreliable, flocking to the side of capital one minute (especially in its fascist forms), the working class the next. In the context of my analysis, however, with its emphasis on size, the role of the old petty bourgeoisie (small businesses and small producers) has to be reconsidered.

21 Karl Renner, 'The Service Class' [1953], in T. B. Bottomore and P. Goode (eds. and trs.) (1978) *Austro-Marxism* (Oxford: Clarendon Press, 1978), pp. 249–52.

22 Cf. Harry Braverman's now classical study (1974) on the spread of detail labour into the 'mental' sphere, previously privileged over the sphere of 'manual' labour. This was the first full-length study of the division of labour within production since *Capital*. Harry Braverman, *Labor and Monopoly Capital: The Degradation of Work in the Twentieth Century* (New York: Monthly Review Press, 1974), p. 329.

23 Gyorgy Lukács, *History and Class Consiousness* [1923], tr. Rodney Livingstone (London: Merlin Press, 1971).

24 Theodor Adorno and Max Horkheimer, *The Dialectic of Enlightenment* [1947], tr. John Cumming (New York: Herder and Herder, 1972).

25 Like Weber, Horkheimer, Adorno and Marcuse thought that the origins of instrumental reason lay beyond industrial capital as such; they also accorded Protestantism a generative place in

instrumental thinking. Max Horkheimer, 'The End of Reason', *Studies in Philosophy and Social Science*, vol. 9, no. 3 (1941), pp. 366–88. Herbert Marcuse, 'Industrialization and Capitalism in the Work of Max Weber' and 'A Critique of Norman O'Brown', in *Negations: Essays in Critical Theory*, tr. J. J. Shapiro (London: Allen Lane, 1964) pp. 227–47. Theodor Adorno, *Negative Dialectics* [1966], tr. E. B. Ashton (New York: Seabury Press, 1973).

26 Ernest Mandel, *Late Capitalism*, tr. J. De Bres (London: New Left Books, 1975), p. 509.

27 Marx in his early writings had discussed this objectification in terms of alienation. Mention of the Marx of alienation perforce recalls the debate about Marx's humanism, but it deserves some attention in this context. Althusser provoked that debate when he insisted that there was an 'epistemological break': between the early and the later Marx. According to Althusser, the early Marx had been a humanist to the extent that he had attributed essential human qualities to human beings, and argued that the process of capitalist production alienated one from one's human essence. Alienation (*Entausserung* and *Entfremdung*), in that it was meant to presuppose a human essence, was thus pivotal in the humanism/anti-humanism debate. In turn, the main critical grounds for repudiating the notion of essence is that it presupposed some naturally given properties, and is to this extent ahistorical, asocial and thus un-Marxist. The later Marx, for Althusser, had dispensed with any notion of essence, arguing that the human being of *Capital* was no more than the bearer (*Träger*) of social relations, a *tabula rasa* before their imposition. Louis Althusser, *For Marx*, tr. Ben Brewster (London: Allen Lane/Penguin Press, 1969). For our purposes it is interesting now that Marx has (at least) two notions of essence (*Wesen*) operating. One is entirely consistent with Althusser's position: 'the human essence is no abstraction inherent in each separate individual. In its reality it is the aggregate of social relations' (Karl Marx, *Theses on Feuerbach* [1845], in K. Marx and F. Engels, *Selected Works*, 3 vols. (Moscow: Progress Publishers, 1969), vol. 1, pp. 13–15 (trans. mod.)). The other notion is closer not to 'essence' but to another of the manifold meanings of *Wesen*, which is simply 'being'. Essence in the sense of being is indeed natural, but it is natural in the broadest possible sense of that term. 'That man's physical and spiritual life is linked to nature means simply that nature is linked to itself, for man is part of nature.' Marx, *Economic and Philosophic Manuscripts of 1844*, p. 68. No specific 'nature' is implied here,

nothing is claimed for, for instance, natural human aggression, competitiveness or some such. What is claimed is that the unalienated life is the life that is part of nature. My argument takes me towards and away from a humanist reading. It runs away from it, for it suggests Marx's reasoning became more anti-humanist than even Althusser allowed. Marx's political economy reveals that will, imagination and goal-direction cease of necessity to be the province of productive labour, to a greater or lesser extent. My position takes me towards the Marx of the alienated essence in another sense, in that it aligns the exploitation and alienation of humans with that of nature. It also emphasizes the relation between large-scale centralization and the foreclosure of opportunities for creative labour. It thus partakes of that general criticism, whose best-known articulation came from the Frankfurt school, of the demise of outlets for human creativity in a system that assaults nature on the grander scale.

28 Like John Locke and others in a line of political theorists and political economists before Marx, Ricardo adhered to a labour-theory of value. But for Ricardo, the value of a particular commodity reflected the particular labour embodied in it, and wages in turn were meant to reflect this value; surplus-value arose through an unfair exchange between labour and capital. The particularity of this definition meant that individual commodities were meant to reflect the value labour added to them, but this meant that it was difficult to see how labour ruled their value, in an overall system dominated by apparently free exchange. Marx overcame this problem with the labour/labour-power distinction: (a) this enabled him to look at profit in overall terms, and move from the particular to the general; (b) the distinction also meant Marx could conclude that capital was not 'unfair': it paid for labour-power at its value. It was just that labour added something more.

29 I have not revisited the debate on abstract labour ('is it physiological or social?') here. I show how it can be resolved in *Your Money or Your Life: The Real Third Way*, Chapter 5, (forthcoming).

30 To complicate this a little, circulating capital also includes the variable capital needed to purchase labour-power. There is here a tacit indication of what I will argue explicitly later in this chapter, which is that all forms of energy, including labour-power, should be treated both as variable *and* as circulating capital.

31 Braverman, *Labor and Monopoly Capital*.

32 Marx, *Capital*, vol. 1, p. 583.

33 In the literature on Marxism and the environment thus far, it has been supposed that if capital has to make provision for environmental safeguards, this will increase the expenditure on constant capital and therefore exacerbate the tendency of the role of profit to fall. Gorz's argument to this effect has been influential. Andre Gorz, *Ecology as Politics* trans P. Vigderman and J. Cloud (London: Pluto, 1983); also Adrian Little, *The Political Thought of Andre Gorz (Routledge Studies in Social and Political Thought, 3)* (London: Routledge, 1996). There may be an increase in constant capital expenditure (especially with environmental taxes), but the greater availability of energy sources offsets it.

34 See Ernest Mandel, *Late Capitalism*. Incidentally, referring back to Chapter 1's discussion of the commodity, it is worth noting Mandel's difficulties with the services industry. Having shown an effect in Chapter 12 that not only circulation in general but the service industry in particular gets completely out of line with any logic of profit, he concludes in Chapter 15 (pp. 454–5) that this is only one instance of the more general disequilibria that mark late capitalism. He insists on the general disequilibria analysis in order to distinguish himself from Friedman's and Rueff's conventional quantity theory (p. 431) although he concedes a 'certain similarity' (p. 435).

35 The concept of a labour aristocracy belonged more to the nineteenth century than the twentieth: Eric J. Hobsbawm, *Labouring Men: Studies in the History of Labour* (London: Weidenfeld and Nicholson, 1964), but the logic remains the same. The labour aristocracy was more likely to perceive itself as middle-class.

36 On the relation between the exploitation of nature and that of people in the non-metropolitan countries, see Michael R. Redclift, *Development and the Environmental Crisis: Red or Green Alternatives?* (London: Methuen, 1984); and Michael R. Redclift, *Sustainable Development: Exploring the Contradictions* (London and New York: Methuen, 1987).

37 This is a distortion of Foucault and Derrida, but it has some currency.

6

PRODUCTION AND
REAL VALUE

The dynamics of how an artificial time is being created are becoming plainer. Energy itself, it seems, is converted into this artificial time. But before these dynamics can be drawn out further, we need to address the other side of that conversion: the depletion of natural substance and energy. With this in mind, I will summarise the main issues facing us in the light of my redefinition of variable capital and the related law of substitution. Given the emphasis on the depletion of nature, this new value-theory seems not to be a value-theory at all, but a theory headed towards the standard economic measure of supply and demand, or availability. It takes us towards that measure as there is no reason for assuming that capital is the least concerned about the reproduction of any natural force, unless it is irreplaceable. And if capital is not intrinsically interested in reproduction then for 'reproduction' we should read 'availability'. That is to say, reproduction is only of interest to capital insofar as it guarantees a continued supply of a natural resource necessary for production. If production can continue through the availability of other natural forces and entities whose reproduction can be disregarded, it is the availability, not the reproduction, that matters.

On the other hand, we now have another way of looking at value-theory, which sees, as Marx saw, the relation between value added in production and the cost of reproduction as the real measure of value. The difference is that this measure has been extended to include natural substances.

This is not to say capital adheres to this substantial measure of reproduction, not for a minute. It is just that this measure will make its effects felt: both in terms of forces that have to be reproduced in the relatively short-term, and in the last instance. Both for some natural forces in the short-term and for all in the long *durée*, the relation between production and reproduction *is* a question of supply and demand: certain natural resources are running out. At the same time, especially in the short-term, the idea that 'supply and demand' has a measure beyond itself is critical:

> Supply and demand regulate nothing but the temporary *fluctuations* of market prices. They will explain to you why the market price of a commodity rises above or sinks below its value, but they can never account for that *value* itself . . . At the moment when supply and demand equilibrate each other, and therefore cease to act, the market price of a commodity coincides with its real value.[1]

The measure of value now becomes, or rather is extended to, the substantial level: energy in production and its reproduction. But the short-term incompatibility of this measure, and that of supply and demand, is another issue, the crucial issue in fact. And it is the issue which shows that value-theory, once its measure of reproduction is generalized from humans to other forms of nature overall, has a long life yet.

The measures of availability and reproduction have to be incompatible in the short term in that capital is also and always governed by time. To get more on to the market in the shortest possible time it has to acquire more at a commensurable speed. Just as we drew out two levels in value-theory in the preceding chapter, one concerned with time and exchange, the other with energy, so we find these levels recapitulated in relation to labour and nature. One is the real level of substance and energy, which determines the time of reproduction. The second, which governs the workings of capital in its day-to-day competitive workings, is the fantasmatic level of time.

Reproduction time, as the real measure of value, intersects with the speed of acquisition to the extent that capital
has to take account of the reproduction of raw labour-power
and, by my argument, of the reproduction of other natural
forces. But if capital can avoid this reckoning, if it can cheat,
it will do so. It cheats by substituting one natural force,
whose reproduction time it can ignore, for another which
it cannot, where the former will do the job, and can be
acquired at greater speed.

Accordingly, the reproduction of labour-power compared
with the value it adds in production must cease to be the
measure of profit in the short term, although it remains the
sticking point, the most obvious reminder of real or substantial value presented by the natural order, as distinct from the
order of speed. I will argue below that the conflict between
these orders is manifest in an increasing distance between
real value, measured by the time of natural reproduction,
and price, measured by speed (another, socially produced,
measure of time). But while it figures, the fantasmatic level
of speed has the overriding power in the short term.

But to argue this, we need a measure of short-term profit,
which is not based directly on the relation between production and reproduction, but which can be tied to this relation
in the long run. We need, in fact, to distinguish between
short- and medium-term profit on the one hand, and long-
term profit on the other. For short- and medium-term profit
I am proposing the speed of acquisition as such a measure;
it will sometimes reflect reproduction time, but it is also
overridden whenever reproduction can be made a non-issue
from capital's perspective.

Acquisition is a term that resonates with the name of
Ricardo. In Ricardo's value-theory, exchange-value embodies
the quantity of labour expended in the acquisition of goods,
as well as their relative scarcity. These two determinants of
value work together; the more scarce a good is, the more
trouble or labour it will be to acquire it. But, of course,
acquisition can demand more or less labour for other
reasons.[2] As with so much classical political economy, as
well as its crasser successors, this is descriptively accurate

up to a point. The point is the intersection of speedy acquisition with the exploitation of substance, and its measurement in terms that reflect that exploitation.

The speed of acquisition, while a slippery variable, is measurable in this way. In itself a measure of time, it is tied to another measure of time: the prevailing or socially necessary time of production. It is the difference between the cost of acquiring raw materials or commodities for production at a certain speed, and the energy they add in production that gives rise to surplus-value. In this connection we can note that labour-power can be exploited in two ways. One is in terms of the energy it adds in production. The other is the fact that it carries the costs of its own speed of acquisition. This two-sided capacity for exploitation makes it hard to replace labour-power as a particular source of energy, aside from its relatively singular capacity for taking direction, and unique capacity for portability. Labour-power can speed itself up.

In proposing the speed of acquisition as the measure of short- and medium-term profit, I am retaining the temporal measure of the original value-theory, the socially necessary time in which a given commodity can be produced and put into circulation, but generalizing it. Socially necessary time is not only 'labour-time'; it is the time within which all natural forces and substances add 'something more' in production, in terms of the technology governing the particular production process in question. Comparable qualifications to all the qualifications that Marx put on labour-time hold here. A hole formed by dripping water is as valuable as one made by water-based electric power, although the former takes a millennium, and the latter a minute.

The speed of acquisition will sometimes embody the cost of reproduction, and sometimes, more usually, not. When it does so, it does so because the general law of substitution is constrained by the fact that the reproduction time of certain natural substances (chief amongst them, but not only, labour-power) forces itself into account. Were it not for this, we could say that the production of exchange-value is the consumption of use-value via the imposition of portability.

But the constraint means that from the standpoint of reproduction time as a general measure, there are two ways of speeding up the rate of surplus-value extraction:

- The first holds for labour-power and agricultural production. It is to allow the natural substance in question to keep its form, but speed up its rate of reproduction (for how this applies to labour-power, see below). However, even when many of these substances and products keep their form, this does not make them exempt from the imperative to speed things up.

- The other way to speed up surplus-value extraction is to speed up the means by which one form of natural energy is converted into another (for instance, coal to chemicals). Now increasing the speed of this second form of conversion leads to ever more rapid means of releasing energy, at the same time as it, of necessity, diminishes nature overall. The full implications of this for profit will be apparent after we show why the quantitative dimension of use-value has to be taken into account.

Here this enquiry branches off into two directions. The first concerns the fate of use-value, meaning nature overall as the source of all value. The second is about the cost and therefore the speed of acquisition as the measure of profit (short- and long-term).[3] I will pursue these two strands to the argument in the next sections, turning first to the overall quantity of use-value, then to how the speed of acquisition intersects with reproduction. We will see that government by the speed of acquisition must work to progressively diminish use-value and eventually real or surplus-value overall.

We can then see how this results in a process where space progressively takes the place of time, and radiates some of its effects on nations, race and gender. But throughout this discussion it should be remembered that these two strands, speed and substance, represent two competing dynamics in any order dominated by capital. Capital will live or die according to the speed of acquisition, but to live by the speed of acquisition is to live under a fantasmatic law. Natural entities and substances will live or die depending on how far their reproduction is permitted, and it is permitted less and less under the law of speed.

As we have shown, Marx insisted that no commodity could have surplus-value or exchange-value without use-value; he also insisted that nature was the source of all use-value, and, with Lucretius, that 'out of nothing, nothing could be created'.

> Use-values are perishable by nature. Hence, if they are not productively or individually consumed within a certain time . . . in other words, if they are not sold within a certain period, they spoil and lose with their use-value the property of being vehicles of exchange-value . . . The use-values do not remain the carriers of perennial self-expanding capital-value unless they are constantly renewed and reproduced, are replaced by new use-values of the same or of some other order.[4]

On the other hand, as also discussed, Marx consigned all natural forces and sources outside labour-power to the dominion of death-sleep. But once they are regarded as variable capital, their consignment to that dead unreproductive place becomes not an *a priori* condition, but a consequence, of the dynamics of production, with quantitative implications for use-value in the determination of surplus-value. Use-value, it will be recalled, is only meant to be a qualitative matter. But this qualitative emphasis is also due to the same subject-centred perspective that led Marx to group nature and things together. He considered the living substances at base of use-value in terms of quality not quantity, because he considered them solely in terms of the ease with which they may be directly consumed by a human. But use-value has a quantitative dimension, to which we have already alluded in terms of a continuum of substance and energy. It is quantifiable to the extent that nature overall is quantifiable.[5]

A convenient way to draw out the quantitative dimension of use-value is to compare agricultural and industrial production. In this comparison we will pretend that agriculture is exempt from the speedy dynamics of capital. In fact agriculture is not exempt at all, but this pretence will help initially to make the point. The point is that subjective agency can either increase or decrease the overall quantity of use-value, the 'small sum necessary for the young man's fortune'. In other words, the capacity for will and design, a capacity that is exercised (at the fullest) by management (or 'non-productive' labour) under capital, can, depending on how it is directed, either increase or decrease the sum of nature. In other modes of production, the human subject is not automatically opposed to nature as one of its own forces. As directed energy, it can either be quantitatively opposed to nature, in that it diminishes its substance, or it can increase the substances in question.

It is not difficult to see how the will enhances or diminishes. For instance, a living tree is capable of producing more trees, and will and design can direct labour in the act of cultivation in such a way that it can transform the conditions of tree production to enable trees to produce still more trees. In this way, it can quantitatively expand natural substances. In the case of the production of commodities in a form in which they can no longer reproduce themselves, the mixing in of labour quantitatively diminishes that substance: a dead tree cannot produce, nor can it be assisted to produce, more trees. One table is usually quantitatively less than a tree.

In other words, whether labour-power quantitatively expands or contracts, natural substances will vary according to the subject of labour-power and the provision made for reproduction. When trees are the subject of labour, they can be cultivated so that they can be harvested for the production of more trees. When timber intended for tables is the subject of labour, the quantity of trees is expanded by labour in order that it may be diminished by it. Similarly, the production of tomatoes quantitatively expands tomatoes in order that they may be harvested, and hence consumed in production. By contrast, the production of tinned tomato soup consumes the tomatoes in the production process as such, in order that they may be directly consumed by the producer.

We have established that the assumption underpinning the theory that profit depends on the socially necessary labour-time required to produce a commodity is that the labourer has raised the use-value of the raw materials to a higher level. The product, through the mixing in of labour-power, is now something more than it was before. In turn, the assumption that underpins this one is that the product is expanded rather than contracted or, to put it differently, that the product is enriched by its transformation through labour-power rather than diminished by it.

Yet from a reproductive, quantitative perspective, transformation can just as well entail that the product's basis is cut back and made poorer.[6] In this case, I think we should borrow Marx's use of the term 'objectification', which he employed to describe what labour *does* in production. We should use it to describe that type of transformation which diminishes, by rendering natural substances into a form in which they are no longer able to reproduce themselves or anything else. This gives us a useful definition of the 'dead' as distinct from the living. The 'dead' is that which either cannot reproduce itself in its original form, or that which can no longer contribute, through its organic decay, to the reproduction of other life. The dead, in this sense, are close to although not identical with those inanimate natural substances which have been produced over the very long *durée* in circumstances impossible to replicate, and whose longevity capital will ignore.[7] Many, though by no means all, natural substances entering production are in this sense 'dead'. As noted at the outset they are removed from the cycles of nature: for this reason, they are on Mammon's side.

Two types of 'transformation' can now be distinguished: that which diminishes and objectifies, and that which does not. This takes us directly to the overall quantitative dimension of use-value and substance. Because, within value-theory as it stands, the energy materialized by labour is only measured qualitatively, because for Marx, this energy was apparent in use-values only, the quantitative aspect to use-values was excluded from the labour-theory of value: no common denominator could be found for them outside of labour-time itself. This means that, from the outset, any consideration of the quantitative matter of the energy materialized in production is precluded, and so, accordingly, is the question of the effects of the increase or diminution of the overall quantity of natural energy or substance capable of releasing energy.

Yet if we suspend for a moment the world in which everything is already a commodity, or destined, as Heidegger would have it, to become such a commodity, if we cease to assume the world of large-scale industrial production, *then surplus-value overall could only increase if the value realized by all the natural substances entering into production was greater than the costs of their reproduction.*

While Marx did not have a concept of the overall quantity of use-value, he did have a concept of overall surplus-value. The concept was demanded by his understanding of total profit. For Marx, overall surplus-value was equivalent to total profit. The justification for this equation rested on the notion of a *total* surplus-value. Surplus-value had to be considered in total terms because determining the price of particular commodities in terms of the labour-time (in terms of the value) embodied in them is unworkable. Capital will move profits around from one sector to another, so that the price of a particular commodity may be more or less than its real value. But these discrepancies will iron out, in that overall profit will equal overall surplus-value extraction. Thus Marx made value equivalent to price in the last (overall or total) instance. We will return to this uneasy equivalence, the problem of transforming value into price, subsequently. The point here is that if there is no surplus-value without use-value. If use-value overall is being diminished, and if overall surplus-value equals total profit, *then total profit in the long run must diminish as the source of use-value overall diminishes.* It could only increase if the literal substance of use-value (the source of all wealth) could realize more use-value, hence surplus-value; that is, it could only realize long-term profit *via* a substantial increase.

But a substantial increase is precisely what capital militates against. It must use natural raw materials more rapidly than they can reproduce themselves. While natural substances, as raw materials, are in fact used to produce a new use-value, they are 'in truth consumed'. From an over-all quantitative perspective, it is inevitable that this form of consumption must in the long run diminish the amount of given raw materials available, in that it diminishes the living natural substances they contain. Unlike feudalism, in capitalism Marx is clear that the amount of natural materials that new productive forces will have to consume must also increase.

> An increase in the productives force ... corresponds to the increase in the instrument, [*Arbeitsinstruments*] since the surplus-value of the instrument does not keep pace, [*entspricht ... in keinen Verhältnis*] as in the previous mode of production, with its use-value ... The increase in the productive forces, which has to express itself in an enlargement of the value of the instrument – the space it takes up in capital expenditure – necessarily brings with it an increase in the material, since more material has to be worked in order to produce more product.[8]

The immediate manifest limits imposed by feudal or other forms of precapitalist production are less immediate and far less manifest. The 'object' no longer imposes direct limits on the 'subject', although its indirect limits are making themselves felt environmentally. But this indirect return of the repressed has been relatively slow in coming to consciousness,[9] and economic formulations of its significance have been even slower in reckoning with the implications of finite quantity for capital overall.

And indeed capital can defer its reckoning with nature, if not endlessly, then for as long as it can find energy sources that substitute for one another. Of course, capital has a very long way to go before it exhausts living nature, and would probably have destroyed the conditions of human survival before reaching that point.

But the issue here is simply that in order to satisfy the demands of large-scale production, more and more of nature has to be destroyed. In this sense production under capitalism is consumption, not production; it gobbles that which is already there, gives nothing back but waste. Its form of transforming labour is not the same as that which marks other modes of production process, in that capital is only concerned about reproducing the natural substances that are the irreplaceable conditions of its own existence, and where these conditions are an immediate condition of its survival. Because so many of the commodities it produces cannot be recycled (in general) or because, if they are agricultural, they tend to exhaust the conditions of their own production (see below), then, given that nature is the source of value, capital can only profit by continuing to exploit every available natural source.

But in this exploitation (nature is given less than nature gives out) we can see that production is not production, but consumption. For transforming production is creation, it is increase in growth, it is the *substantial* increase, the increase in substance. Consumption, on the other hand, diminishes, unless it is geared to reproduction. If labour, as energy generated by nourishing matter, in turn assists the growth of nourishing matter, then consumption is directly related not only to production but to the reproduction of the conditions of consumption. But under capitalism, consumption bears no relation to production, except in its own terms, and these must diminish the quantity of use-value overall to the extent that speed is capital's imperative. The embodiment of energy in the fixed forms of constant capital not only reflects a process whereby the organic composition of capital changes, with more spent on constant, less on variable, capital. It also reflects a diminution in the overall quantity of use-value: the energetic substances bound in fixed capital are no longer able to reproduce themselves.

The world of subjects and objects expands at the expense of the logic of natural substance.

But what needs to be stressed now is that surplus-value does assume a material embodiment. In fact, this was clear on the micro-level the minute we drew attention to the incidental energy capital acquires in its contract with labour-power. The concept of surplus-value draws on both use-value and exchange-value; we signalled this by making the two-fold nature of the commodity our point of departure. But this two-fold nature also means that surplus-value, conceptually, mixes up use-value and exchange-value. The confusion over surplus-value is compounded, and may have arisen in the first place because the quantitative implications of consumptive production were neglected. This much is now clear: as far as the long term is concerned, as the overall quantity of substance or use-value is diminished, so must the overall quantity of potential surplus-value, and hence profit, be diminished. What remains to be discussed is short- and medium-term profit, which leads us once more to the speed of acquisition, hence to time.

Notes

1   Karl Marx, *Value, Price and Profit* [1865], in Marx and Engels, *Selected Works*, vol. 2, pp. 31–76, p. 45.
2   David Ricardo, *Principles of Political Economy and Taxation* [1817] (London: J. M. Dent, 1973).
3   One of the problems with any discussion of profit in relation to Marxist political economy is the elision of profit with productivity. Sraffa drew out the different bearing of both concepts and was thus able to give a working solution to the transformation problem. Piero Sraffa, *The Production of Commodities by Means of Commodities: Prelude to a Critique of Economic Theory* (Cambridge: Cambridge University Press, 1975). Cf. Anwar Shaikh, 'Marx's Theory of Value and the Transformation Problem', in J. Schwartz (ed.), *The Subtle Anatomy of Capitalism* (Santa Monica, CA: Goodyear, 1977), pp. 106–39.
4   Marx, *Capital*, vol. 2, pp. 130–1.
5   Effectively, this means that the overall quantity of nature is equivalent to the technological ability to conquer and exploit the space of the infinite; and of course we keep pushing at the limit implied.

6   Ted Benton, 'Marxism and Natural Limits'.
7   These inanimate things are not identical with the artificial death imposed by many forms of commodification in that they also contribute to the reproduction of organic life by their ecological input.
8   Marx, *Grundrisse*, p. 380.
9   Although not as slow as popular writings have it. Environmental consciousness has been present to some degree since the seventeenth century. Cf. Richard Grove, 'The Origins of Environmentalism', *Nature*, 3 May 1990, pp. 11–14.

7

THE SPEED OF ACQUISITION, OR HOW SPACE REPLACES TIME

By this analysis, for production to continue to stay in the race, it has to speed up the materialization of energy, the value added by natural substances in production, and so speed up the rate of surplus-value extraction. While this speeding-up diminishes overall surplus-value in the long term, it obviously works compellingly in the short term. The question becomes *how* does it work? Let us return to the two ways of speeding things up. One is allowing a natural force or source to keep its form, while speeding up its rate of reproduction; the other is to speed up its conversion into energy by changing its form.

(i) On nature keeping its form

If we treat all natural forces capable of materializing energy, or commodities produced naturally (agriculture), as variable capital, the problem with the idea of nature's expanding use-values, and therefore expanding the potential basis of exchange-value, would appear to be not that natural substances lack the 'specific' quality of labour (for materializing energy, thereby increasing value), but that they cannot be measured according to the socially necessary labour-time for, say, a plant to produce a tomato. This, as noted, is a problem for agricultural capital in particular, in that agricultural commodities are more obliged to keep their form. Yet it is not an insurmountable problem.

It will be recalled that the concept of socially necessary

labour-time is based on the average amount of time required to produce a given object at a given level of technology. Now the average amount of time a tomato plant takes to produce a tomato can in fact be calculated with some precision. The real point is that the plant's technology *appears* or *appeared* to be fixed. Marx obviously lived in the era before genetic engineering. Accordingly, he assumed that the reproductive time of natural substances cannot be speeded up; that is, the tomato plant's inner working cannot be regulated or controlled. It is historically plain that this is not so, and that capital has indeed found social ways of speeding up various forms of natural reproduction.[1]

The speeding-up of the natural products which need to keep their forms in order to serve as agricultural commodities takes place by regulating their conditions of production. These commodities generally are animals, animal products, trees, plants and their produce. We have succeeded in breeding pigs without trotters that cannot walk. They lie on shelves to speed up the fattening that takes them to pork; cows are next in line for the same treatment, and wingless chickens are on the way in.[2] 'Modern turkeys have been bred with breasts so large that it is impossible for them to mate.'[3]

There is no doubt about the motive, not even a coating of palaver about science for science's sake. Simply, 'a wise farmer is not going to buy a patented animal, or any other item, unless it will increase profits. That is just what transgenic breeds are being engineered to do'.[4] The chickens already lay eggs at several times the natural rate under battery lamps; the lactation of cows is artificially increased; and the tomatoes, like a great deal else, are planted in soil which has been artificially fertilized to mean its fallow time is by-passed. For that matter the plants themselves are subject to genetic recombination guaranteed to increase their rate of reproduction.

By the processes that speed up the commodification of animals and plants (amongst other things), surplus-value will be increased, but the longer-term effect may well be an impoverishment of surplus-value based on use-value, to the extent that surplus-value must embody use-value. I say 'may well be' because it is always possible to take account of the conditions of use-value production (for example, replenishing soil fertility by natural or artificial means). However, if we keep our focus on the overall quantity of use-value, then this account-taking must either diminish the overall quantity or run counter to it if it is done naturally. If it is done naturally, it will be at odds with the speed imperative. If it is done artificially, and being done at a profitable speed, it must be overdrawing somewhere else.

The price paid for speeding things up is a price paid by overall productivity, and hence overall long-term profit. There should be a decline in long-term profit to the extent that commodities embody less real substance, and this they must do as they become degraded of substance. Take the giant, airy American strawberry. Genetically recombined for improved size, and grown in degraded soil, it looks great and tastes . . . like nothing. In the medium term, even its comparative price has fallen. It is a symptomatic postmodern commodity: seeming wonderful, yet it has literally less substance, and hence less value. None the less, its price increased in the short term with the speed of its deceptively luscious production.

(ii) Changing the form

Short-term gain and a decline in long-term productivity and profit are also evident in the second way of speeding things up, characteristic of industrial production: changing the form of natural forces and sources beyond recovery. But they are evident at an even more accelerated pace. Changing the form of a natural force or source can involve violent conversions whereby, for instance, coal is converted into electrical power or naturally occurring organic compounds are reproduced in artificial conditions, or recombined in chemical conversions to make anything ranging from plastic to CFCs.

Noting these forms of speeding up surplus-value extraction may help us unravel the Marxist conundrum of transformation, of how value is transformed into price. In doing so, it may also reconcile some of the insights of mainstream economics with Marx's alternative.

Within industrial production the necessary natural forces have to add more at a faster speed, within less time, than the time in which they are acquired. This puts a fantastic temporal pressure on all aspects of capital's circulation and production.[5] To hold its own, a particular capital has to acquire its energy sources (along with everything else) at or better than the prevailing speed.

The fact that this fantastic temporal pressure affects all aspects of capital's circulation and production means that the speed of acquisition, as a measure of profit, involves distribution and exchange as much as production. This runs counter, of course, to the classical account, precisely because that account downplays circulation. Which is not to say that the *interdependence* of the four spheres of classical Marxism (production, reproduction, distribution and exchange) has been understated. But the fact that they become direct actors in the production of surplus-value has been understated. They become direct actors once the focus is on the speed of acquisition as a key to surplus-value. Moreover, and this will become increasingly significant, they are direct actors who show that the state, as the entity which provides 'the general conditions of production',[6] is, or at least has been, inextricably intertwined with capital. What is more, they draw attention to the importance of space and distance as capital speeds up.

The role of space and distance is evident once we consider the variables affecting the speed of acquisition. In discussing this, I will use the more neutral term 'cost' in the first instance. The cost of acquisition depends on: (i) how many stages of transformation a living entity or substance has to go through before it acquires the form desired for consumptive production; (ii) the distance of the entity or substance from the place of production, and thus on (iii) the means of transportation, whether they exist or have to be constructed (an additional cost) and (iv) whether the cost of means of transportation or of utilizing them, where they exist, is stood by capital. In all cases, all measures of the cost of acquisition are spatially as much as temporally relative measures; this is where the cost of acquisition becomes equivalent to the speed of acquisition, however distant from the real value inherent in the time of reproduction that cost may be.[7] Finally, and most significantly, the cost of acquisition also depends on (vi) whether the reproduction cost can be discounted by capital.

The burden of this argument is that the reproduction time, or real value, will be and is discounted as industrial production grows in scale. Discounting the cost of reproduction, in fact, is the other side of centralization and globalization alike.[8] It is not only quantitatively, in terms of use-value, that these processes demand more of nature than they can return, to support a political, juridical and distributive apparatus additional to those essential for local production. It is also that the pathways of centralization and globalization are simultaneously the pathways of any extended acquisition. In one respect, this was anticipated by Marx:

> The *smaller* the direct fruits borne by *fixed capital*, the less it intervenes in the *direct production process*, the greater must be this relative *surplus population and surplus production*; thus, more to build railways, canals, aqueducts, telegraphs etc. than to build the machinery directly active in the immediate production process.[9]

I return to spatiality, centralization and the global state below. Enough at this point that centralization (both in larger reproduction conglomerates and in urban centres) demands that greater distances be covered; globalization extends this process further. What I want to suggest now is that the costs of distance, in the speed of acquisition, are what sets the 'price' as distinct from the value of a particular commodity. While Marx noted that the price of a particular commodity need not embody its labour-time, he did not identify any particular factor which had an overriding power in the determination of price. I do not dispute that many things can remove price from value. But I am suggesting that distance has a special role, sufficiently special to mean that we need some way of calculating its effects on profit. Thus tentatively, I am suggesting that the effect of distance on the spread of acquisition is the major, constant factor in the determination of price[10].

The considerable advantage of reading value-theory in terms of interchangeable energy sources is that it means we can account for distance as a factor determining price in a way that ties it to reproduction; it ties it to reproduction in so far as distance substitutes for reproduction. In more detail, I am proposing that distance figures in this way: the speed with which all commodities are acquired in production in Department 1 (Marx's term for consumption for production) and distributed in Departments 2 and 3 (the arenas of individual consumption) consumes energy. Precisely because the surplus-value released in this consumption is not measured against the time of reproduction, but against the speed of acquisition, then price becomes further removed from value, literally removed. And price becomes higher the less the time allowed for reproduction. Paradoxically, the less the time allowed, the higher the price, because allowing for less time means that more surplus-value is released. In other words, the price is higher the greater the extent of centralization and globalization, the more distance has to be covered at a higher speed, the more energy consumed, and the less the return to nature.

But if price is set by the speed of acquisition, value remains tied to the time of reproduction: the time of the natural and social reproduction of natural substances. In many instances and for some capitals, depending on their location and their ability to outlay, the measure of value will figure more markedly and, accordingly, be closer to price. It will figure necessarily in agricultural production, especially those forms of it which rely relatively little on inputs from afar. Speed ramifies here, as we have seen. But it does so mainly through speeding up production. And, of course, reproduction as a source of value matters more to the extent that production relies on labour-power. This will explain why the labour-theory of value appears to work by some accounts, particularly those based on case studies of neo-colonialist countries. It is when and only when the cost of reproduction can be discounted that the value added in production is to be compared not with the cost of reproduction, but with the cost of acquisition.

The 'when and only when' is crucial. It keeps the basis of value-theory, in recognizing nature as the source of all use-value, and hence of value; therefore, it does not partake of capital's crazed capacity to lose track of value's source. At the same time, this 'when and only when' embraces the fantasmatic escapism of production based only on the cost of acquisition, which is the main basis that capital, and the economic theories which best describe it empirically, acknowledge.

Of course, energy cut off from its natural source of origin cannot continue to regenerate the natural energy that enabled it to come into being. However, as more and more natural substances are cut off, and as more and more natural substances are bound in fixed capital, they require more and more supplies of external energy to enable them to keep producing, due to the obvious facts that they are both diminishing the overall quantitative supply of nature and that they have no regenerative energy of their own. However, as capitalism cuts back the supply of natural substances, it not only diminishes nourishing matter – one source of energy – it also diminishes the conditions for other natural sources of energy to regenerate as well. So it has to speed up agricultural production. Speeding up agriculture in turn feeds into the speed of acquisition through consumption, which depends on wide networks of distribution, as does industrial production.

In fact, this is where the two forms of speeding things up are tied together. To acquire more at a faster speed for production means distributing more and consuming more. This puts a pressure on agriculture to produce at a rate comparable with other aspects of production and distribution. As available sources of energy in either agriculture or industrial production are diminished, capital has to create routes for the old sources of energy to come from farther away, or create new sources of energy altogether, ranging from electricity to chemicals to 'nuclear power'. But if the logic of consumption for production holds here, then 'nuclear power' should also be exhausting something. (What?)

Leaving that aside: the reproduction of natural substances and sources of energy goes according to a natural cycle taking a certain amount of time. The hyperactive rhythm of capitalism, on the other hand, means that the conversion of substances into energy leads to the further conversion of already converted substances into other energetic forms, which are more and more coming to be the basis of energy overall, with lunatic environmental consequences. As by now should be abundantly plain, the reality of what we should relabel the consumptive mode of production (CMP), or 'capital' as we will continue to call it for the time being, is this: short-term profitability depends on an increasing debt to nature, a debt that must always be deferred, even at the price of survival.

As I indicated, distance should bear on inflation. Money, as Alberti claimed long before modern economists did so, is essentially time. Marx measured money in terms of labour-time, but by this argument it should be measured in terms of the speed of acquisition. Thus inflation and interest would be the measures of distance between sources of energy and the speed with which they are consumed, a measure which intersects with reproduction, especially but not only that of labour-power. We will regard money, then, as the phenomenal form of the socially produced time of speed, rather than of labour-time as such. This retains some of the reasoning behind Marx's definition of money, although that definition conflated the social time of production with natural reproductive time, and it is these we are separating in this redefinition of the relation between value and price. The price of a commodity becomes inflated the further removed it is from its value, and especially inflated if its production has removed the source of value altogether. The price of money, measured in interest, would be affected by the same variable. Once more, time, as money and speed, literally encapsulates the natural energy whose flourishing it must diminish. For if the quantity of use-value overall as the basis of surplus-value is diminished, as I have argued it must be, something has to take its place. This something is the creation of an artificial space-time. This creation is the means whereby money rivals natural time in its imitation of reproduction.

Short-term profitability, with its inflated price, must lead to a diminution in long-term profit and productivity. In that the substantial material embodiment in productivity and profit has to be reduced or rendered unreproducible by the logic of production geared to speed, capital is its own worst enemy. How this is played out in total terms should be reflected in the crisis of capital, in its 'long waves' and 'laws of motion'. In sum, what Marx saw clearly and before all was the inherent contradiction in capital as a mode of production. He saw it in terms of labour and technology, or constant and variable capital, as he defined it, where the former, to keep pace, had to expand at the expense of the energy input of labour. The contradiction is recapitulated in this account, although its terms of reference have changed. Or rather, its terms of reference have been stripped of their phenomenal forms, so that the contradiction emerges as what it is essentially: one between substantial energy and artificial speed.

Yet we have established that the contradiction between energy and speed is not simple. Two forms of time are at issue: the generational time of natural reproduction, and speed, the artificial time of short-term profit. Speed, as I have already indicated, is about space as much as time as such. It is about space because it is about centralization and distance. Speed, measured by distance as well as time, involves a linear axis, time, and the lateral axis of space. In what follows, I will begin by emphasizing how, in the consumptive mode of production, the artificial space–time of speed (space for short) takes the place of generational time. For to the extent that capital's continued profit must be based more and more on the speed of acquisition, it must centralize more, command more distance, and in this respect the artificial space–time of speed *must* take the place of generational time.[11]

It is clear that generational time suffers because capital tends inevitably to speed up the production of all commodities, including naturally formed or agricultural ones. While there are countervailing tendencies in agriculture and labour-power, in terms of scarce or apparently irreplaceable sources, the speed imperative will override them wherever possible. As production speeds up, it is also clear, capital will diminish or degrade the conditions of the specific or overall natural reproduction of natural and agricultural products. But this is not the only way that generational time is short-circuited by short-term profit.

As I have indicated in relation to fixed and constant capital, capital will also bind more and more living energy in forms which cannot reproduce themselves. The same is true of many commodities produced in Departments 2 and 3: commodities for the individual consumer's consumption. These fixed or bound commodities either cannot be recycled at all, or are out of time in that they can only be recycled at a pace far slower than that of other biospheric ingredients. The production of these kinds of commodities is the heart of industrial production, and this industrial heart has a temporal beat which was noted at the beginning of Part II: the beat of instant gratification, a beat that gets more rapid by the minute. The substances in bound commodities are cut out permanently from the generational process of natural exchange at the same time as they are inserted, in their newly acquired objectified or bound forms, into the process of commodity exchange. Of course, it matters to some substances more than others; trees lose more than rocks or minerals.

But what these erstwhile natural things lose in their ability to go on living, to reproduce down the generations, they gain in mobility. Not much of a gain, to be sure, for the things themselves, but a big gain for capital, which certainly requires the portability of commodities. Moreover, one cannot consume more products within production without having a market for those commodities outside production. So both processes of consumption have to be speeded up. The more directly consumable a product is, the greater its use-value. Once more, the easily consumable product is the one that is most portable, and that involves the least expenditure of energy in consumption (a dish-washer is more valuable than a bucket; and infinitely more valuable than a stream; a micro-wave meal costs more than the same ingredients brought separately and prepared). More time and energy are required to produce these products and make them portable; less energy to consume them, especially if they come to you, and come to you as fast as possible.

In short, a commodity has to be shiftable, for it has to be able to come to market. Aside from pigs and their ilk, commodities can only come to market in a movable form, and this means that they have to be shifted, i.e. removed, from the circumstances in which they can reproduce themselves. The exceptions here are labour-power and animals. I noted that one of the distinctive features of the commodity labour-power is that it is portable of its own accord. Not only that, but human beings, like other animals, can be transported without losing their capacity for reproduction. But humans and animals aside, no other natural substance can reproduce itself if it is uprooted, or, more generally, removed from the earth. However, centralization requires portability and therefore uprooting; and it requires it more the faster production becomes, and the more the scope of centralized production extends. This should mean that, until and if something takes its place in a cost-effective way, the portability of labour-power becomes ever more important, both as a commodity which covers its own transportation costs, and because of the part it plays in shifting things around. And the scope of centralization must extend as the extent of acquisition depends on it.

As we have seen, to extend acquisition one needs means of transportation in the first instance: either to bring the desired good to you, or for you to go to it. Extending acquisition to consume more goods in the process of production auto-matically entails two things. The first is an alteration in the scale of production. Production ceases, to a greater or lesser degree, to be local in scale, and this means the consumptive producers are more likely to lose track of the source of value, in terms of the time of natural reproduction. The second consequence of extending acquisition has also been discussed, but I need to restate it as we are coming closer to the base role of the global state in the process whereby time is made over in favour of space. The second consequence of extending the means of acquisition is that the speed with which the goods have to come to the point of production also increases. That is how capital operates according to its own fantasmatic law of speed. Or rather, that is the operation of the process we are renaming centralized consumption, a process of which capital is the greediest and most efficient exemplar. The more things are brought together from out of their habitat and locale, the more networks bringing them to the place of consumption are needed. The more they are brought together, following the paths of centralized consumption, the more they are cut out of their habitat and locale. The more they are cut out, the less they can reproduce. The less they reproduce, the less they become. The less they become, the more substitutes for them need to be found. The more substitutes need to be found, the greater the globalization needed to find and transport them. Centralization, speed and spatial scope all increase because the newly produced goods have to be produced and distributed in accord with a timescale that at least matches that of local production in order to compete with it, a timescale that will of course aim at overtaking local production and same-scale competitors.

In other words spatial centralization creates energy demands and an energy field which can only sustain itself by extracting surplus-value from nature. It is impossible for it to do otherwise: even without the imperative to constantly speed up to stay in the races, the additional demands large-scale extension makes on the reproduction of nature, through transportation and energy services (electricity, water and so on) means that more has to be extracted from nature than can be returned in terms of the time necessary for natural reproduction. This form of extracting surplus-value from nature is inexorable, for it maintains the *centralized* apparatus of state and global trade and communication networks *and* advanced technological production.

Thus the distance of production and distribution based on

the increasingly large-scale extension of capital takes the place of time. Moreover, distance should take the place of time in inverse proportion to it, so that generally, lateral space will more and more substitute for the time of local generational production and consumption. Space will take the place of time by the denominator common to both: namely speed, and it will take time's place by increasing the speed at which the entities and substances traverse the means of transportation to the place of production, the speed with which they are consumed in production, and the speed at which they are distributed, in accordance with the scale in which they are consumed in production, and distributed for further consumption.

This speedy continuum of consumption for production and further consumption is the essence of why space has to override time in the CMP. In fact, the idea that spatial extension of itself demands that more be extracted from nature than can be returned demands a formula: the condensed distance and imposed directions of spatial extension are paid for by the time necessary for natural reproduction. I am tempted to postulate another law here, to the effect that what any natural thing loses in terms of its ability to reproduce, it gains in portability. It was with this in mind that I suggested earlier that where the speed of acquisition is unimpeded, the production of exchange-value is the consumption of use-value, via the imposition of portability.

We are left with a world in which centralized and globalized space, in general, is paid for by the sacrifice of reproductive, or generational, time. This world is made over on a lateral axis, which uproots to a vast extent the generational or 'linear' one. In this making over, capital carries on like a parody of natural production. Not only does it like to produce plastic oranges, Stepford Wives, and other imitations of the original; it has to have a means to 'reproduce' its products, to enable substance to turn into something else. In natural reproduction, this is the energy generated by the natural cycles themselves. And we know that capital, like nature, uses energy to enable it to transform one substance into another. But it garners its energy by violent conversions, and these conversions follow rhythms that bear only an attenuated relation to the rhythms of natural production, whose temporal constraints they ignore.

In reproducing or producing its babies, capital has its own cycles and 'laws of motion'. Its parody of nature is almost complete. It plays God and redirects nature at its own speed and from its own subject-centred standpoint. It is playing with high stakes here, because it is literally altering the *physis* of the world, adjusting the inbuilt logic of nature and the spatio-temporal continuum to suit itself. By its will, it is imposing a direction on physical processes which is other than their own. As it creates this subject-centred world of objects, and the artificial pathways and laws of motion that reform the natural connections it breaks, it makes a fantasy come true. It establishes its own foundations, but it does so by consuming the real foundations, the logic of natural substances. Meantime the wilful subject, the agency affecting this, becomes more and more invisible in the diverse forms of power without accountability that mark the present era.

We return to the alteration of the *physis* towards the end of Part III. Before that, taking account of the speed factor, as the intersection between the linear axis of time, and the generational axis of spatial reproduction, will enable us to say something brief about: (i) the state; and (ii) the reproduction of labour-power and the positions of women and men, especially in the neo-colonial context.

Notes

1 While in this section we are talking of substances which need to keep their original form, and probably their ability to reproduce themselves, in order to serve as commodities, it should be remembered that the same process applies to some natural substances capable of materializing energy as such (e.g. oil seed).

2 The outstanding account of genetic engineering and biotechnology is Jeremy Rifkin's *The Biotech Century* (San Francisco: Trager/Putnam, 1998). Relevant information can also be found in animal rights bulletins. For more information on this topic, see Pat Spallone, *Generation Games: Genetic Engineering and the Future for Our Lives* (London: The Women's Press, 1992),

especially; also Arno G. Motulsky, 'Impact of Genetic Manipulation on Society and Medicine', *Science*, vol. 219 (1983), pp. 135–40; V. G. Pursel, C. A. Pinkert, K. F. Miller *et al.*, 'Genetic Engineering of Livestock', *Science*, vol. 244 (1989), pp. 1281–7; and Roger Straughan, *The Genetic Manipulation of Plants, Animals and Microbes* (London: National Consumer Council, 1989).

3 L. J. Raines, 'The Mouse that Roared' [1991], in F. Grosveld and G. Kollios (eds.), *Transgenic Animals* (London: Academic Press, 1992), p. 341.

4 Ibid., p. 342.

5 It is a pressure consistent with capital's behaviour, as we shall see below. As noted at the outset, time, in general, is more likely to be central in most non-Marxist economic theories. But these theories discuss time without reference to an overriding source of value. Marx explicitly notes that:

> A capital's time of circulation . . . limits, generally speaking, its time of production and hence its process of generating surplus-value. And it limits this process in proportion to its own duration . . . But Political Economy sees only what is *apparent*, namely the effect of the time of circulation on capital's process of the creation of surplus-value in general. It takes this negative effect for a positive one, because its consequences are positive. It clings the more tightly to this appearance since it seems to furnish proof that capital possesses a mystic source of self-expansion independent of its process of production and hence of the exploitation of labour, a spring which flows to it from the sphere of circulation . . . Various phenomena . . . give colour to this semblance: 1) The capitalist method of calculating profit, in which the negative cause figures as a positive one, since with capital's indifferent spheres of investment, where only the types of circulation are different, a longer time of circulation tends to bring about *an increase of prices* (Marx, *Capital*, vol. 2, p. 128–9, emphasis added).

Marx regarded this increase as equivalent to the process of equalizing profits extracted through exploitation for surplus-value. And there is a sense in which I am saying the same thing, in arguing that value has to be consumed as distance is covered in any form of circulation. However, value has been generalized to the exploitation of nature overall, and the suggestion is that the 'increase of prices' is tied directly to the consumption of use-value, via the speed of acquisition, where no allowance is made for the time of reproduction. On the transformation problem more generally, and attempts to rework it, see Sraffa, *The Production of Commodities*; Shaikh, 'Marx's Theory of Value', pp. 106–39; Geoffrey C. Harcourt, 'The Sraffian Contribution: An Evaluation', in Bradley and Howard (eds.) *Classical and Marxian Political Economy: Essays in Honor of Ronald L. Meek* (London: Macmillan, 1982); and Geoffrey C. Harcourt, *Post Keynesian Essays in Biography* (London: Macmillan, 1993).

6 Marx, *Grundrisse*, p. 533.

7 At the same time, if one of production's elements can be had more cheaply, this may have the same effect as speeding up: the end result will be a lower cost, although the benefits here may be offset if there is a time-lag in the speed of production, thence distribution. The relativity of cheapness, in other words, is relative to the absolute of the prevailing speed of production and distribution.

8 It is their logical concomitant, just as the division into town and country is the concomitant of industrialization.

9 Marx, *Grundrisse*, pp. 707–8.

10 Up to a point, this coincides with the 'primitive' definition of value, which defined the value of commodities in terms of their distance. See Marshall David Sahlins, *Stone Age Economics* (Chicago: Aldine-Atherton, 1972), especially Chapter 5, 'On the Sociology of Primitive Exchange'. Cf., too, C. Gregory, 'Gifts to Men and Gifts to God: Gift Exchange and Capital Accumulation in Contemporary Papua', *Man*, vol. 15, no. 4 (December 1980), pp. 626–52, and Mary Douglas and Baron Isherwood, *The World of Goods* (New York: Basic Books, 1979).

11 The same point is very well made by Elmar Altvater, 'Ecological and Economic Modalities of Time and Space' [1987], tr. M. Schatzscheider, *Capitalism, Nature, Socialism*, no. 3 (1989), pp. 59–70, in the context of a discussion of thermodynamics, economics and time. This article is in part a creative, critical discussion of Georgescu-Roegen's thermodynamics-oriented 'bio-economics' (which argues, on the basis of Newton's second law, which it applies to space, that scarcity is inevitable). Georgescu-Roegen differentiated between time 'T' (a continuous sequence) and time 't', the mechanical measurement of intervals. Mechanical time lacks the historical sense that goes with a continuous sequence, and it is also opposed to historical time 'T', because it cannot be measured and predicted mechanically. For Georgescu-Roegen, 'a particular logic develops in the space and time coordinates (as in the social and economic

coordinates): economic surplus production is guided by the quantitative imperative of growth by way of reducing the time spans of human activities (especially those of production and consumption). It does this by accelerating and transcending the quantitative and qualitative impediments in space in order to compress time, thus setting 'T' into 't'. There are thus two coordinating systems of space and time, which, in the form of two patterns of 'functional spaces', are fixed upon a territorial-social reality.' Altvater, 'Ecological and Economic Modalities', p. 63. Altvater goes on to conclude that 'the expansionist pressure inherent in the economic logic or surplus production has a territorial dimension (as production is necessarily always spatial). Surplus production is thus identical to the economic conquest – exploration, development, penetration and exploi-tation – of space, i.e. the 'production of space'. Ibid., p. 69.

Part III

POLITY

The theory advanced in this book has sometimes been misunderstood as metaphysical or idealist. In fact it is neither.
'Idealism' presupposes a distinction between the ideal and
the material, a distinction I have argued against both here
and elsewhere, on the grounds that to conceive of ideas as
unphysical is to fall into the logic of foundational thinking.
Moreover, the idea that the foundational fantasy exists on the
large scale, that its effects and ambitions are not reducible to
human agency, means that the subject is most certainly not
the source of all agency and meaning, any more than there
is a realm above and separate from the physical. The project
here is bringing Lucifer and his opposition down to earth.
The foregoing reworking of the labour theory of value is
based on an epistemology which showed that the distinction between subject and object rests on and reproduces
ingrained categorical habits in which mind and body, ideas
and matter, are conceived separately. I mention this because
my economic arguments are sometimes treated as if they
could be separated from the epistemology underpinning
them.

But it is one thing to disavow a superstitious or metaphysical stance, another to show that the theory that results
from refusing to split sacred and physical laws and concerns
has more explanatory use than one that does not. If my
reworking of value theory is right, it should cast explanatory light on the reproduction of labour, hence on women,
race and class. It should also bear on the political sphere:

economic expansion, globalization and nation states. In the next chapter, I will try to show that this is so. However the bearings I sketch are speculative; they are not based on an empirical overview of the extensive literatures in these fields, although they can be measured against those literatures. In Chapter 9 I return to the question of scale in a political and historical context. Scale is critical in this theory, precisely because it relies on interpreting the hubris of modernity in terms of a relation between macrocosm and microcosm. The extent to which the foundational fantasy takes hold psychically depends on the extent of its material enactment. It follows that attempts at symbolizing or linguistically figuring alternatives to the fantasy will fail without alterations in economic scale. This is because the economic dimension is the key to the increasing materialization of the fantasy.

Chapter 9 discusses this in relation to the question of the fantasy's universality, as well as in relation to the question of scale. This necessitates a brief discussion of the historical aspects of my claims, which in turn leads into a discussion of the construction of imaginary time. The focus here is on the *physis*, the interaction between microcosm and macrocosm, and how the sense of history is constructed as things get faster and faster. The last chapter is about exploitation and the various forms of opposition to the ego's era. The reader interested in what is to be done may wish to read this chapter first; it follows on directly from Chapter 8's concerns with the applicability gap, and the question of who gets to be in the right place at the right time.

8

THE STATE AND
EXPLOITATION

It is becoming increasingly clear that the momentum of capital alone is insufficient to account for the power of agency, the true 'invisible hand', in the spatial extension process described above. I have noted that centralization is inextricably tied to the state, which provides 'the general conditions of production'. The more the emphasis shifts to portability and acquisition, and the more by implication it shifts to expansion, the more the issues of territorial control, guaranteed economic access to territories beyond given borders, and transportation (those vague 'conditions of production' Marx refers to) become salient. To extend centralization, and territorial access and domination, one needs means of transportation in the first instance, trade agreements in the second and for domination, means for war.[1] Spatial control and spatial expansion are the conditions of the invisible hand extending its grasp.

The state is part of the infrastructure of distribution, the outer sphere of consumption and exchange, all of which are not peripheral but central in my revised value-theory. Not only does the state lay the grounds for and regulate key variables in the speed of acquisition: (through transportation, energy services, trade agreements and other forms of extension). Together with capital it also regulates the law of substitution. For example, whether oil can substitute for labour-power in the production of certain commodities will depend on means of transportation, treaties governing import, and so on.

While the costs of establishing centralized state control in the first instance, and globalization networks after that, may not be of particular significance to use-value overall in themselves, they are none the less paid for out of that use-value, and consume it in the same way that capital does. While Marx noted that the state provides the 'general conditions of production', he did not note the remarkable structural homology between these 'general conditions' and the requirements of production, let alone that 'production' is also a means to the state's self-expansion. Yet the homology is becoming increasingly apparent, although it is usually described as a trend. Thus Mandel:

> There is . . . an *inherent trend under late capitalism for the State to incorporate an ever greater number of productive and reproductive sectors into the 'general conditions of production' which it finances.*[2]

This homology is, or was, striking in a recent stage of capital's development: state-monopoly capitalism, so-called because the mutually supporting interests of both parties seemed so great as to beggar separate description. But however unwillingly it did so, the state provided the spatio-temporal conditions of production from the beginning. In one respect, the periodisation of the various 'stages of capitalism' in Marxist theory is incomplete because it does not recognize that the establishment of the modern state is integral to the historical process whereby space takes the place of time. The existing periodisation moves from competitive capitalism (first stage) to monopoly capitalism (second stage) to state monopoly capitalism, otherwise known as late capitalism (third stage). But the third stage reveals the spatial imperative in all its munching glory, with its speedy circulation and its ever expanding reach that cuts off the roots of reproductive time. This imperative gives us globalization as well. There is now an ongoing debate as to how far globalization is a fact, and how far capitalism and production are constrained by nation states.[3] Of course both things are true. Capital is constrained within states. At the same time, this reworking of value theory has shown that profit depends on a spatial *dynamic* of extension and acquisition, with the demand for ever more fodder, a demand which must press beyond national borders in executing the process of leveling time. In addition, as we will see in a moment, while all states feed on time to some extent, as their infrastructures take more from nature's reproduction than they return, they vary in the efficiency and extent to which they do so, and in the constraints that their various cultures and histories impose upon them. This variation is reflected in the uneven demise of state power, and states for that matter. The demise suggests that while the nation state was one form in which 'the conditions of production' were laid down, it may not be the only form that will sustain them.

Crucial here is the idea, as Wilcox argues, that standards of efficiency in denying time are set globally. For Gourevitch, it was a global economic pressure in the 1980s that made nations 'curtail state spending and interventions. Whatever the differences in partisan outcomes, all governments have been pressed in the same direction'.[4] Even more strongly: 'governments no longer possess the autonomy to pursue independent macroeconomic strategies effectively, even if they were to seek to do so'.[5] Moreover, it is argued that today state power should not be measured in terms of military force but economic capability[6] and, at the same time, that the states' domain of economic efficacy is now shared with many international organizations (e.g. the IMF).[7] Hall, Held and McGrew, in an excellent discussion of this literature from which my examples are drawn, stress that while this economic direction may be a global trend, not all states are affected equally.[8]

One reason why they are not affected equally is this: while any form of state will embody the spatial dynamic to the extent that it has an apparatus of centralized control, some states embody it in a purer form than others. Indeed some states are constrained by other imperatives which make them manifestly inefficient when it comes to speeding up the sacrifice of time. This is where the effects of specific genealogies, specific traditions intersect with those of the

totalizing spatial process. Britain, which is generally inefficient when it comes to traversing space, exemplifies well the
conflicts between spatial extension, and a tradition which
gives too much weight (however misplaced) to generational,
temporal rights: social position determined by birth, respect for
queues, etc. although this respect may fade as time gives way.

More dramatically, the collapse of Eastern Europe can be
explained by the conflict between a form of state, and the
dynamic whereby space replaces time, and the related desire
for instant gratification. We will come back to this briefly
below: the fate of Eastern Europe and the plight of the former
Soviet Union indicate why the spatial dynamic is the overriding one.

We have to bear in mind the different roles various states
play in providing and regulating general conditions where
space replaces time. Marx's analysis of how some states aid
accumulation and expansion better than others[9] is appropriate here as an exemplar of how the modern state can be
evaluated, albeit by different criteria. Some states are far
better suited than others to the law of speed, and where the
state fails to adjust its form to this law, or attempts to
countermand it, there will be gigantic temporal hiccups.
The form of centralized state which naturally works in
harmony with the process of acquisition, and thence distribution, is a state with minimal checks on the abolition of the
linear time of reproduction in relation to labour-power, and
in relation to the environment.

This last point returns us to the reasons for blockages in
the former Soviet states. I am unable to deal with this
question in detail here, or with reasons for the collapse of
the ex-communist societies, but I will make some brief
suggestions in the hope that another will either refute or
verify them. If my economic theory were to be applied to
Eastern Europe, this is what should follow. State commu-
nism, in so far as it did attempt some minimal redistribution
of wealth to labour-power (which means to its reproduction
cost), imposed a temporal constraint on a system designed
to eliminate it; for any system of centralized consumption
must work towards increasing speed in relation to space

rather than time, and this is a concomitant not only of competitive acquisition but of spatial extension. If a state has to introduce some guaranteed measure of distributive justice, this inevitably leads to hiccups if not major obstructions: distributive justice, as we shall see in a moment, is a temporal constraint which can be offset where labour-power is imported, but it remains a temporal constraint when it is honoured.[10] It sits ill where the elimination of time and instant gratification are the end-goal of the game. It becomes unobtainable where expenditure on an arms race is also demanded.[11]

The question of distributive justice and temporal constraints will be plainer after we have discussed reproduction, which bears on women and neo-colonialism. As with the state, the key to the following perspectives is the intersection of space and time. More narrowly, it is in how this intersection, itself established by speed, brings in the sphere of reproduction, especially of labour-power. For while my argument displaces labour-power from the absolute centre of value-theory in terms of production, it also shifts the emphasis to labour-power's reproduction, as it shifts it to that of nature overall. To a limited extent this shift was foreshadowed in debates about women's (domestic) reproductive labour, which investigated the notion of this labour's *indirect* contribution to surplus-value. But this debate foundered because it kept within the classical categories.[12] The shift to reproduction in this argument is structural. Reproduction of nature overall becomes the hidden ground of value and exploitation; capital drastically enhances its profit because it does not pay for reproduction at its temporal value, unless it has no option under the law of substitution.

From the perspective outlined above, the reproduction of labour is the perpetually odd element out in production. Labour-power is the odd element because the socially necessary labour-time required to reproduce it is fixed in part by nature. It is fixed in so far as socially necessary labour-time includes the reproduction of children and thus the next generation of labour-power. While the time necessary for the reproduction of nature, even of animals, can be short-circuited, that of labour-power cannot, on the face of it, be speeded up, which means such reproduction is potentially out of step with capital's consumption-for-production, in which all things have to move faster and faster.

Now as the imperative to speed up other living entities and substances is so evident in everything from soil poisoned with fertility-drugs to wingless chickens and legless cows, animals tailor-made to producing flesh at the expense of their own ability to reproduce, human labour-power's apparent exemption from the same speedy imperative becomes significant. But, always in the event that no other natural substance can provide what labour-power provides (the law of substitution), the apparently impossible end of speeding up the generational reproduction of labour-power can be accomplished in various ways. It can be accomplished by keeping the cost of that reproduction down in relation to the other elements entering production. However, if this means is ineffective in a given situation, where the labour required exceeds the short-term supply, then one is left with the apparently impossible alternative of speeding up the generational reproduction of labour-power so that it keeps pace with the other elements entering into production.

In fact, speeding up the reproduction of labour-power is not impossible, and this is plain once we turn to the alternative means by which human labour-power can be reproduced. In referring to 'alternative means' of reproducing labour-power, I am not invoking the panoply of science fiction and high-tech, of cyborgs and genetic engineering, although the proliferation of fantasies concerning the former and investment in the latter is not irrelevant. In part, it is perhaps a symptomatic recognition of an underlying quest to find a fast-moving replacement for humans, capable of what we distilled as their most distinctive functions: portability and the capacity to take direction. For that matter, all the carry-on over artificial intelligence has more obvious purpose and point, if capital seeks a tame direction-taker. And, of course, such docile will-less things already exist, in the form of computers, which in their literal-mindedness altogether lack what Marx called 'imaginative capacity for design' in executing commands. But the computerized component in constant capital expenditure, and the ambition it encapsulates, is not the immediate question. The alternative means of reproducing labour-power I have in mind at the moment is what I will term the lateral reproduction of labour-power, meaning the migrations of workers.

What I want to propose here is that the lateral reproduction of labour-power will increase when the linear reproduction falls behind the imperative to speed up in other ways, and/or when linear reproduction becomes too costly. At the same time, I want to propose that such increases work in tandem with an imperative to keep the cost of the generational reproduction of labour-power down, in lieu of the ability to speed it up. These propositions could be tested readily enough, keeping the law of substitution in mind. And in so far as they encapsulate the law of substitution, it should follow that where the lateral reproduction of labour-power is prohibited for some reason, the generational cost of reproducing labour-power will be forced down.[13]

Clearly, these processes involve international labour flows as well as national labour supplies, and national legislation affecting the cost of reproducing the next generation. All these are regulated by the state. And it should follow that a good welfare state will either be 'inefficient' or have ready access to guest workers; a state without this access will 'speed up' generational reproduction by keeping its cost down. The condition of an efficient and just welfare state is either that it is self-contained enough to keep to economies of scale, and/or that its natural resources make it rich provided they can be exploited fast enough (but substantially rich in the long run anyway). We can note here that the former Soviet Union was restricted when it came to importing labour-power. The production of surplus-value in a country which disregards a welfare state is enhanced anyway, of course, but enhanced either by speed or natural substance and energy: the USA is rich in natural substance, while Japan led the field of speed (until money and currency manipulations within the sphere of speed and artificial time – initiated in the US – set it back).

To return to reproduction as such. We are left with the question as to why people have children at all in these speedy times. In feudal and petty-bourgeois modes of production, the interests of social reproduction and the interests of parents coincide. In capitalism, they do not coincide automatically,[14] which means that the overall interests of social reproduction are not guaranteed; they are not in the necessary self-interest of either sex. The striking facts of the increase in single mothers and decline in fathered families may evince this conflict with self-interest for men.[15] But we are unable to explain women's persistence in having children in terms of self-interest, especially as the middle-man is progressively cut out. We can only explain this, and explain the behaviour of men who want children, by (at least in part) their resistance to the economic logic of self-interest, and their persisting sense of generational time. Symptomatically, it was argued by the right that there is an economic self-interest factor working for *women* who have children, and receive a state benefit. But this seems unlikely.[16]

What is clear is that the interests of social reproduction overall are best served by keeping the costs of the linear and lateral reproduction of the labour force to a minimum. This means that two groups are likely to be impoverished: single women and/or women who are positioned low on the class spectrum (see below); and the vastly heterogeneous peoples from whom a lateral supply of labour-power can be drawn. If there is a structural connection between gender, race and the residual category of class, I suggest that this is it. In other words, the structural connection lies in their exploitation for social reproduction, for keeping the cost of labour-power down. These forms of exploitation prop one another up.

The heterogeneous peoples who supply the migrating labour-force are far more likely to be those who are racially and ethnically stigmatized. Wallerstein and Balibar sum up:

> Racism operationally has taken the form of what might be called the 'ethnicization' of the work force . . . But while the pattern of ethnicization has been constant, the details have varied from place to place

and time to time, according to what part of the human genetic and social pools were located in a particular time and place and what the hierarchical needs of the economy were at that time and place. This kind of system – racism constant in form and venom . . . allows one to expand or contract the numbers available in any particular space-time zone for the lowest paid, least rewarding economic roles.[17]

There is more incentive to migrate where there is unemployment or bare subsistence employment in the home country, and/or where there is overpopulation relative to job supply. The international interests of reproduction by the nations of advanced capital would seem to be well served by overpopulation in the neo-colonialist countries, both in terms of a greater willingness on the part of the latter's populations to migrate, and in terms of greater competition for jobs within those countries.

Significantly, it is usually men who migrate or move in search of work,[18] while women with children remain fixed in place. This repeats a pattern evident in capital's seventeenth-century genesis, and in the non-metropolitan countries where capital's advent is relatively recent.[19] This pattern goes hand in hand with a major alteration in scale. It is not only the division between town and country that is affected here; it is also the household, as the site of production.[20] Household production, or petty commodity production, as Marx and Engels termed it, accorded women a very different and generally better economic place. Their productive labour was not geographically divorced from their situation as mothers.[21] The significance of household production for women has been relatively neglected in Marxist debates about whether petty commodity production is a precapitalist form or an on-going form of capitalism.[22] The idea that it may be a form opposed to it was proposed by Clark,[23] but her remarkable thesis was not developed.

But the immediate concern lies elsewhere. Apart from indicating that the production of migrating men and single mothers is endemic to and a condition of capitalization, this pattern also reinforces the notion that these two groups have a great deal in common. They have in common their exploitation for social reproduction, even though their short-term interests are opposed. Or, to say the same thing differently, they stand opposed in that one group advances lateral reproduction, the other linear reproduction.

In this context, we can reconsider the concept of class. This is now a problematic concept. It has been thrown into question especially by the debates and research which point to an increase, in the advanced countries, in the size of the middle class.[24] It has been put into question here by the realignment of productive labour with nature. Earlier, I laid out grounds for arguing that the increase in size and the realignment of labour with nature were related. If nature is also a key source of surplus-value, then it would be possible within an economy overall (when its profit or surplus-value is conceived in total terms) for more people to live literally off the fat of the land, and the oil, and the sea, and the beasts, and even the genetically modified lilies of the field. But where that is not possible, or less possible, 'people' will occupy the same position as nature, exploited at the level of production as they are at reproduction. In terms of production, they will be positioned like the will-less other of the foundational fantasy; they will be those who serve more of themselves and their energy than they are served, those who are denied agency in production while they run down their bodily being.

Taking this more slowly: as noted above, traditionally Marxists have defined class in terms of whether or not labour is productive. The working class is productive, the bourgeoisie or ruling class unproductive, and debates have raged over the productive status of the petty bourgeoisie and/or new middle class. I have argued that productive labour is that which is closest to other natural forces and sources, in terms of its inability to exercise will and design, direction and control of the production process. We have also seen that this inability is tied to scale; it is as production becomes centralized that the labourer loses a direct and imaginative relation to the product. We can add here that even after industrialization, it is women who are most significantly affected by the scale factor. In most sectors of the economies in England and France 'the smaller the scale of organization, the larger the size of the female workforce'.[25]

But, by this argument, scale, centralization and distance have figured in the production of surplus-value in another way: surplus-value is also measured against the speed of acquisition, which consumes energy: the energy of labour and other natural forces. I have also suggested that distance figures here, in terms of speed (how far the commodity to be consumed in production or outside it has to travel, and how fast, affects the energy consumed). And I have argued that surplus-value produced this way works on a different axis (space, related to price) from surplus-value produced by comparison with the time of reproduction (value).

The question becomes: where class is concerned, how does surplus-value measured by the speed of acquisition intersect with surplus-value measured by the time of reproduction? Remembering that labour-power is both a commodity that is consumed in production, and one that consumes, we can begin answering this by noting that the speed of acquisition has been tied to a continuum of consumption, in an argument which makes consumption for production and further consumption integral to the production of surplus-value.

In this version of value-theory, social reproduction has become a means of adding value in itself. It has become this means precisely because of the emphasis on energy consumed in distribution and exchange, which of course involves the energy consumed by and in the reproduction of labour-power, both at the level of day-to-day consumption, and of generational reproduction which is where, most obviously, women's domestic labour adds value. Moreover, on the axis of acquisition and consumption and from capital's perspective, labour's voluntary portability marks it out from other living substances, whose transportation and distribution costs are stood by capital. We have seen that in terms of the lateral and linear modes for extracting surplus-value, labour-power provides a surplus in both respects. It adds value in the traditional way. And in covering its own transportation costs, it decreases price.[26] But does this make for a necessary tie between portability and productivity? Within the framework of the old value-theory it does, in that labour-power's transportation costs are part of its own social reproduction costs, which have to be less than the value it adds in production. On the one hand, making social reproduction a value-adding variable in itself means that there is no necessary connection between traditional productivity and portability. They are both axes of exploitation. But when portability and reproduction are united, as they are here, as different sides of acquisition, portable labour-power is connected structurally to the 'fixed' reproducers of labour-power.[27] This structural connection solves the problem set out by Balibar which is how 'to keep "in their place", from generation to generation, those who have no fixed place . . . For this, it is necessary that they have a genealogy'.[28]

It is married women who stay fixed in place, and often suffer more economically by doing so.[29] Their fixity here overlaps with, and is reinforced by, the fixing of a negative image onto them which we discussed in Part I. The individual energetic exploitation works with the social one. But, once again, the same is true for ethnicity and race: the offloading of a negative image and the aggression that goes with it onto the different other establishes a fixed point with energetic gains to the colonist. The difference is that these ethnic and racial 'fixed points', when they are masculine, are free to move at the economic level. More accurately, they are frequently compelled to move. Their portability is often a condition of their survival. In both cases, enforced fixity or compulsory migration, the result is economic anxiety – the other side of the aggression that secures the subject's position. In other words, those who are positioned as objects are the repositories of anxiety, who benefit the subjects, who project their aggression onto others without suffering the effects of aggression in turn. But there are very few people today with so much power that they can avoid all manifestations of aggression.

The elusiveness of such people is the main reason why it is difficult to make more remarks about class position, especially middle-class position. I am very aware of this difficulty and, in truth, think it arises because class as defined by Marxism is disappearing, but exploitation as defined by Marxism is not. I suppose one can say, schematically, that the ruling class can be defined as those who have maximum control and design of production, and whose social reproduction costs are entirely covered by surplus-value. True subjects they. But one can say nothing so schematic about the vast new middle class. We can note, however, that this class has been tied to the massive growth of the service industry,[30] which may give it a special connection with the foundational fantasy, which I analysed in terms of commodities which seek to serve. In addition, the notorious instability of the middle-class and, for that matter, all who dream under capital, is exacerbated by the scrabble for the subject's position, to be the one who secures it, who is able to project fixity and delay and aggression onto the other. It is exacerbated by the way the foundational fantasy shapes consumption desires regardless of class position.

In a loose sense, it is obvious that consumers are divided into classes in terms of their ability to consume. In fact this ability is a significant if unreliable indicator of class position. It is also an indicator in the spatio-temporal terms which are fundamental in this rewritten value-theory, and it works in the following way.

The less the delay the consumer endures between desiring the object of consumption and acquiring it positions that consumer in spatio-temporal terms by definition. The commodity that comes to you is more expensive, and your class position will appear more substantial if you can afford to have commodities come to you. If you can, or if you choose to seem as if you can, you act out the foundational fantasy more dramatically as a subject. This level of consumption – Departments 2 and 3 – is now evidently homologous with Department 1: instant gratification prefigures and demands speedier acquisition; the speed of acquisition makes for more instant gratification.

Of course the range of objects desired will be circumscribed in terms of what is fantasized compared with what is realistic, and this circumscription is precisely what makes the spatio-temporal indicator of consumption unreliable. In an economy which fosters credit, and whose permanent inflation can only be explained in relation to credit (by Marxist and non-Marxist economists alike), the delayed gratification that marked capitalization in its reality-testing heyday is increasingly undermined by the way in which money, as credit and interest, measures the speed of acquisition in terms of price. Today you can have it now and pay later, and consumers are exhorted to do just this. Whether you can actually afford to have it now, but nonetheless *have* to have it now, are questions which need not be decided by income, provided credit is good. For this reason the limits on delay, in an increasingly fantasmatic economy, are set by the limits on credit. These limits are often countermanded by the credit masquerade, a masquerade of phenomenal marks of 'class'; they are also countermanded by aspiration. An aspiration, a dream, if not a goal-directed course towards being in the position where it all comes to you: this is probably the single most important factor disrupting and undermining any class solidarity or class definition.

Consumption reveals the homology between the individual foundational fantasy and the broader socio-historical process. More generally, we now have grounds for showing how a proliferation of economic, social fixed points works hand in hand with the repressed psychical ones. But before returning to the foundational fantasy, note that there is now an inescapable connection between the exploitation of the environment and the process of surplus-value extraction.

The object which makes a profit is the object which controls the environment, in terms of speeding it up and moving it round, creating its own 'laws of motion'. In addition, we are able to see that the aim of capital is to create the conditions by which it is in fact able to control the environment. To a certain extent, it is successful, and its success is the condition of its profit. *Mutatis mutandis*, the object which makes a profit *has* to be that which controls the environment, remembering that this control has a very specific content. It is a content far more specific than that given 'control' by Heidegger, because of the precise way that control is geared towards speeding up time and collapsing space. I have given an account of the mechanism by which time, measured by delay, is progressively eliminated. This mechanism is surplus-value extraction, usually known as profit, which in the portable world it generates breaks down the constraints that kept Mammon in check. It does so not only in terms of class and sex-identity patterning, but in terms, which we can now see are related to class, of the extent to which fantasies come true and gratification comes more rapidly.

As Weber saw so plainly, a temporal shift, of a different but related order to the one the state effects, was crucial in capitalization. This was Protestantism's shift towards delayed gratification. While this shift appeared to take account of time, it did so by retaining a surplus extracted, in the final analysis, from generational time. Calvinism *conserved*; it did not throw its bread upon the waters, or anywhere else. But unlike today's subjects, the subjects of Protestantism were prepared to wait. The ability to delay gratification has now become the desire for instant gratification, with many means for that desire's gratification, if you occupy the right position in the right place.

Notes

1 If one doubts that speed of portability is a cardinal fantasmatic axis in capital and associated forms of foundational 'self-expression', one need only note the line which, to vary Adorno's metaphor, led from the portable troops on the straight Roman road to the portable nuclear missile.

2 Mandel, *Late Capitalism*, p. 484.

3 Paul Q. Hirst, *From Statism to Pluralism: Democracy, Civil Society, and Global Politics* (Bristol, PA: UCL Press, 1997). John Gray, *False Dawn: The Delusions of Global Capitalism* (New York: The New Press, 1998). Hirst shows that the extent of globalization is exaggerated; Gray shows that it is happening. Both studies are excellent and not in fact incompatible, once one takes account of how different polities resist or reinforce the trend to spatial extension.

4 Peter A. Gourevitch, *Politics in Hard Times: Comparative Responses to International Economic Crises* (New York: Cornell University Press, 1986), p. 33.

5 G. Garrett and P. Lange, 'Political Responses to Interdependence: What's "Left" for the Left?' *International Organization*, vol.45, no.4 (Autumn 1991), pp. 539–64, p. 543.

6 Richard N. Rosecrance, *The Rise of the Trading State: Commerce and Conquest in the Modern World* (New York: Basic Books, 1986); Robert Jervis, 'The Future of World Politics', *International Security*, vol. 16, no. 3 (1991), pp.39–73; Joseph S. Nye, *Bound to Lead: The Changing Nature of American Power* (New York: Basic Books, 1990).

7 Robert Cox, *Power, Production and World Order* (New York: St. Martin's Press, 1987); Martin Shaw, *Post-Military Society* (Cambridge: Polity Press, 1991).

8 Stuart Hall, David Held and T. McGrew (eds.), *Modernity and Its Futures* (Cambridge: Polity Press, 1992), p. 91, and see Paul Q. Hirst, *From Statism to Pluralism*.

9 Marx, *Capital*, vol. 1, p. 751.

10 Of course the collapse of Eastern Europe is a question for detailed study, but I will make some more very general remarks here. The more highly developed technology of the advanced heartlands is inextricably bound to a higher level of surplus-value extraction from natural substances overall. *In principle*, provided the country has enough natural wealth, this means that labour-power need not be exploited as much as it would be in the absence of that technology: there is no need to increase the rate of relative surplus-value extraction to countermand the expenditure on constant capital. Just as this makes the immiseration of the working class less likely in such societies, so may it increase it in societies without the same technological outlay *if they lack natural wealth*. Lesser technological outlay and fewer natural energy sources should lead (via the law of substitution) to increased pressure to exploit labour-power. But as labour-power has to be paid, and as it cannot be seriously overworked in an ostensibly socialist economy, then relative surplus-value extracted from labour-power can only be increased through degrading its sphere of consumption. In terms of the psychical dynamics discussed above, this must increase consumer aggression, the demand for choice, and so on.

11 It also signals a tension between the size of state and communities which constitute themselves as economic and political entities on different scales.

12 With two exceptions the main contributors to this discussion all

argued that women's domestic labour benefited capital. J. Harrison, 'Political Economy of Housework', *Bulletin of the Conference of Socialist Economists*, vol. 3, no. 1 (1973); Maria-rosa Dalla Costa, *The Power of Women and the Subversion of the Community* (Bristol: Falling Wall, 1973); Christine Delphy, *The Main Enemy* (London: Women's Research and Resources Center, 1977); Jean Gardiner, 'Women's Domestic Labor', *Bulletin of the Conference of Socialist Economists*, vol. 4, no. 2 (1975). The problem was that if surplus-value depended on productive labour, and productive labour did not take place in the household, then how did women contribute to it? Jane Humphries, 'Class Struggle and the Persistence of the Working Class Family', *Cambridge Journal of Economics*, vol. 1, no. 3 (1977), in an outstanding historical study, argued that domestic labour was actually a support in and to working-class struggle, and that the working class was worse off if both spouses laboured outside the home as well as within it. See also Teresa Brennan, 'Women and Work', *Journal of Australian Political Economy*, vol. 2, no. 1 (1977), pp. 8–30, for a similar argument based on migrant women in Melbourne industry. The discussion in Michèle Barrett, *Women's Oppression Today: Problems in Marxist Analysis* (London: Verso and New Left Books; second edition 1988) gives an overview.

13 Etienne Balibar and Immanuel Wallerstein, *Race, Nation and Class: Ambiguous Identities* (London: Verso, 1988), p. 108.

14 The birthrate in the advanced heartlands of capital is declining while that in the neo-colonialist countries increases. These trends are at odds with demographic predictions which see a fall in birthrate as consequent on industrialization and agricultural modernization, no matter where and under what circumstances that industrialization and modernization take place.

15 See the discussion in B. J. Elliot, 'Demographic Trends in Domestic Life 1945–87', in David Clarke (ed.), *Domestic Life and Social Change* (London and New York: Routledge, 1991), pp. 85–108.

16 While the publicity given feminism may beguile us into thinking otherwise, the overall global *economic* situation of women *viz-à-viz* men appears to have declined during the twentieth century.

17 Balibar and Wallerstein, *Race, Nation and Class*, pp. 33–4.

18 Louise A. Tilley and Joan W. Scott, *Women, Work and Family* (London: Methuen, 1987), p. 77.

19 Tilley and Scott's classic study puts a general thesis on the effects of industrialization in the family economy, but concentrates on England and France in its detailed study. Their general

thesis is borne out by the non-metropolitan studies; the path-breaking work here is Ester Boserup, *Woman's Role in Economic Development* (New York: St Martin's Press, 1970). Another significant early study here is Irene Tinker, 'Women's Place in Development', in Summary of Papers presented to the Society for International Development, Fourteenth World Conference, Abidjan, Ivory Coast, August 1974. For an update see Geraldine Reardon, *Power and Process: A Report from the Women Linking for Change Conference, Thailand, 1994* (Oxford: Oxfam, 1995).

20 Linda J. Nicholson (ed.), *Feminism/Postmodernism* (London: Routledge, 1990), p. 3ff.

21 One of the striking and most impoverishing effects on women as mothers wrought by industrialization was the event of the putting-out system. This meant women could work at home but without the protection of the social structure of the family economy or union regulation. Tilley and Scott, *Women, Work and Family*, p. 75.

22 A. M. Scott, 'Rethinking Petty Commodity Production', *Social Analysis*, vol. 20, special issue series (1986). Michael R. Redclift and Enzo Mingione (eds.), *Beyond Employment, Household, Gender and Subsistence* (Oxford: Basil Blackwell, 1985).

23 Alice Clark, *Working Life of Women in the Seventeenth Century* [1919] (London: Routledge and Kegan Paul, 1982).

24 Karl Renner, 'The Service Class' [1953], in T. B. Bottomore and P. Goode, eds. and trs., *Austro-Marxism* (Oxford: Clarendon Press, 1978), pp. 249–52.

25 Tilley and Scott, *Women, Work and Family*, p. 68.

26 At the phenomenal level, this is a marker of class. Those who are furthest from the place of production, those with longest to travel of necessity (without, for example, parking places, etc., provided) are those lowest down the class scale. If you are adding more value than you get, if your means of subsistence are less than the energy you transmit in the process of production, you are probably covering your own transportation costs. If you are the consumer of labour-power, and therefore are non-productive in the technical sense, labour-power is a commodity that is desired and comes to you. Moreover, as capital, as a purchaser of labour-power, you will choose the labour-power which comes to you readily at least cost, rather than standing the costs of flying, or in other ways transporting your labour to the point of production.

27 Despite attention to sexism and the invisible support of household labour earlier in their joint study (Balibar and Wallerstein, *Race, Nation and Class*, pp. 34–5), Balibar and Wallerstein do not

refer to sexism when discussing how the contradictory requirements of destabilization and maintaining fixity are to be met. Ibid., p. 212. None the less their identification of these two contradictory aspects to capitalist accumulation is of critical importance.

28 Ibid., p. 213.

29 On the different impact of industrialization on married and single women, see Tilley and Scott, *Women, Work and Family*, p. 88, and Ann Douglas, *The Feminization of American Culture* (New York: Avon, 1977), p. 56; see also Katrina Honeyman, *Women, Gender, and Industrialization in England, 1700–1870* (New York: St. Martin's Press, 2000). Most women were married, however, and the research on this inclines to the view that women's position deteriorated more than men's, although the real contrast of course should not be with the position of men, but between women's position before and after capitalization. Tilly and Scott's comparative study supports the idea that the position of women invariably suffers (both in relation to their former position and in relation to men) with twentieth-century 'development' and capitalization. Clark's sociology of women in seventeenth-century Britain supports the same conclusion. So does Boserup's study of the effects of development on women in Africa. For a contrasting view: Ginsborg argues that it was the migrating men who suffered most in the Italian *miracole*; unlike the women, they lost the support of the traditional kin networks. Paul Ginsborg, *A History of Contemporary Italy: Society and Politics 1943–88* (Harmondsworth: Penguin, 1990).

30 Renner, 'The Service Class'.

9

IMAGINARY TIME

The desire for instant gratification ramifies throughout this argument. We have seen that it is not only a psychical or personal matter, but an economic and historical phenomenon. In this and the following chapter I will revisit instant gratification, and how it affects the perception of time. I will do so, first, in terms of the psychical and historical issues raised at the outset; second (Chapter 10), in terms of the physical, energetic issues raised throughout this book. In both arguments, I am assuming that the modern reign of Mammon is born of patriarchy.

In one respect, the tie between modernity and patriarchy should be plain enough: it is there in the fact that the apparent object of the foundational fantasy is the mother. In another respect, I have not given this assumption enough attention, and will attempt to remedy that in this chapter. By patriarchy, I mean a system of social life which moulds the foundational fantasy into an acceptable expression, at the same time as it fosters some of its fonder delusions. To the extent that this book offers a theory of history and modernity, this notion is fundamental. It is basic to the political and ethical implications of my argument. For if the psychical affinity between modernity and its patriarchal sire is forgotten, it is relatively easy to mistake the constraints that feudal patriarchy imposed for solutions to the anomie and fragmentation that mark postmodernism. The longing for the past, the seeping nostalgia that character-izes key theories critical of the modernity that leads to postmodernism, is prompted and then justified by a limited insight, limited in that it sees the patriarchy that preceded this era and kept it in check as its solution, not its precipitate. Lacan's own understanding of the ego's era,[1] the notion of the culture of narcissism,[2] the belief in the corrosion of the lifeworld,[3] all imply that we should go back to patriarchal hearth and home.[4]

We reach other conclusions if we retrace the relation between the foundational fantasy described in the first two chapters and its patriarchal enactment. By the foregoing account, the ego comes into being and maintains itself partly through the fantasy that it either contains or in other ways controls the mother; this fantasy involves the reversal of the original state of affairs, together with the imitation of the original. The reversal of positions is where the child takes the mother's place in fantasy and imagines that the mother is a baby who depends on it. But it imitates the mother from its own standpoint, a standpoint in which control and power are motivating forces. The reversal of positions, or the wish to reverse positions, is the second response to the unpleasant reality of dependence. The first response is to deny that the mother exists at all. When recognition of the other is unavoidable, the ego's first response is that it is not the dependent child. In patriarchal societies, the fantasized reversal of the original state is actualized to some extent in the relation between the sexes. Herein lies the importance for a man of the need to take care of the other, to be the breadwinner, a matter whose significance may lie in the distance between the extent to which he actually gives of himself, and the extent to which he relies on the other's giving him an image of himself as giving, regardless of the reality of whether he gives or not. Patriarchal societies reinforced the fantasy of controlling the mother, whose capacities they denied in theory. This theoretical denial (while it was contradicted by the practice of premodern women) laid the grounds for denying any notion of indebtedness or connection to origin. During the seventeenth century the reversal of the original state took this denial to its fantasmatic conclusion. Not only was the mother's creativity denied; she was also meant to be the infant's devoted servant. Wet-nursing and the freedom it gave biological mothers were decried at exactly the point where the liberal demand for equality was proclaimed. There is no better illustration of how the demand for equality may contain within itself the Luciferian desire for control.[5]

Any patriarchal system which accords sole creative agency to the father, or symbolizes creativity solely in the father's name, partakes of that denial, however much it might think it works against it. A patriarchal religion might be reckoned a wise cultural compromise in that it also 'contains' denial by its very acknowledgement of the creative power of God, but the price of denying the mother is that the denial of dependence is inbuilt even when it seeks to combat this denial in other ways. To say this is not to advocate that the father be denied as the mother has been. The point rather is to recognize how the denial of the mother initiates the process of the denial of indebtedness as such. In addition, as one might expect given the historical specifity of the denial of energetic connection, there is also a related historical dimension involving an increasing failure to symbolize the feminine divine. As we have seen, until the second century, the doctrine of the Trinity allowed the divine mother a place. And as we have seen, until the second century, following the Hebraic tradition, the holy Spirit, termed *Ruah*, was feminine.[6] This third member of the Trinity is also, in the Catholic Liturgy, the 'Giver of Life'. Life, once more, is the creative force opposed to death and envy alike. It is a force, whether in its immanence in nature or in the capacity to give birth, that is maternal.

The denial of maternal origin marks a patriarchal society. But the truly patriarchal society (not the same thing as sexism, not in the least) is on the decline. And as it dies out, denial of the maternal persists and extends its reach, via the imitation of the original embodied in commodities, and the nature-consuming conditions of their production. Any strategies, let alone solutions, thus begin with recognizing the explicitly maternal nature of the origin that is denied. But while they begin there, they do not end there. The construction of sexual difference along patriarchal lines is not the origin of the foundational fantasy. Rather it seems that, in patriarchal societies, a far more ancient conflict is played out in the arena of sexual identity.[7] How universal this conflict is, is another question; so is the question of whether the fantasy is inevitably patriarchal in its expression. As these questions bear on the historicity as well as the political implications of this argument, they need to be considered.

By this argument so far, there is good reason to place the foundational fantasy well before its technological reinforcement. But there is also good reason to limit any claims about the fantasy's historical generality. The fantasy is evidently historically and culturally variable, and probably historically restricted in the sense that the opportunities for acting it out are restricted, if not positively interdicted by religion and law. Alternatives to it were symbolized in the premodern West, and are symbolized in other cultures. Generally, this alternative symbolization features in cultures which are not marked by extensively technologized and urban, built environments. In these cultures, production is local in scale, the relation to nature physically closer. This is not, it never is, to reduce symbolizing alternatives to local scale and closeness to nature. It is, however, to stress that thinking and experiencing oneself as an energetically contained system is more likely in a culture in which fixed points proliferate. It is also to stress, simply, that alternatives to this and other elements of the fantasy *can* be symbolized, and this fact reminds us that psychical being and ethical possibilities are not confined to foundationalism. We are always more than that, but the circumstances in which we become something more, and the duration for which we sustain that becoming, are constrained by the interactive economy (in all senses) and the fixity of the environment we inhabit.

I will review the constituent elements of the foundational fantasy to make this clearer, turning first to the subject/object distinction. The idea that this is universal, and the related preference for visual and 'object'-oriented thinking, is also highly dubious. The distinction comes to power under the same circumstances as the notion of energetic containment although, like that notion, it long preceded the technological circumstances favourable to it. An enlargement of scale does not *produce* subject/object thought, but it does enhance its dominance. Other elements in the fantasy have more claims to cultural universality, although they vary in intensity.[8] The factors of envy and sadistic aggression are presumably universal this side of paradise. The more specific desires to devour, poison and to dismember also have good general claims, as do the ethical codes which forbid these desires' naked expression. But the desire to dismember or destroy *in order to know* is something else. As with much else in the Faustian repertoire, this seems Western. The desire for instant gratification, the desire to be waited upon, the envious desire to imitate the original, are more troubling, in that their universality is more difficult to locate. At one level, imitating the original is as universal as children playing parents,[9] and men imitating mothers at one remove.[10] But whether envy is a necessary corollary of imitation is questionable. Imitation can also be accompanied by envy's opposite: admiration. We might say that imitation can be gauged envious where the original is denied, by any of the mechanisms of denial (from trivializing to trashing). The desire to be waited upon is manifest in any assertion of power which involves the one's *going to* the other. But the close relative of this desire, instant gratification, again seems heavily culturally modulated in Western terms.

In sum, some elements of the fantasy are universal, although their strength can be reinforced or negated. On the other hand: first, the desire to know by dismembering and destroying; second, the subject/object thinking which is tied to hallucinatory envious denial; and third, instant gratification, or the denial of time in relation to power and control, seem slanted to the West. These are also precisely the desires that are most reinforced in constructed technological inertia. The shift from a genuinely patriarchal feudal society to a sexist capitalist one is also the shift from a society with a limited technology to one that is capable of satisfying the desires in the foundational fantasy with more precision. Thus it is more likely that psychoanalytic case histories will uncover the desire to poison the mother (read: nature), rather than revere her in the infant psyche of today. But that the desires existed beforehand is not open to doubt. A few other remarks on their proliferation, and their aims, are in order.

The less technologically efficient or controlling the culture, the less nature can be denied as source, although it can certainly be railed against. There has been more railing in the West than outside it; in some non-Western cultures, nature can also be symbolized with something like affectionate regard, a partner to be worked with rather than feared and subjugated.[11] However, the same regard need not be extended to women. Joint expressions of the desire to control the mother and control nature again keep harmonious company in the West especially, as does the wish to make both mother and nature passive while becoming the agency of control. The explicit idea of indebtedness, however, meaning the acknowledgement of an origin to which one owes one's existence, features in any theistic or deistic culture, which means all cultures other than a predominantly middle-class section of the culture (broadly conceived) in which I am writing. Obviously there is no corollary between acknowledgement of the mother's creative agency and believing in creative agency as such. None the less, there is a corollary between denying the mother's agency and denying creative agency *tout court*. This is apparent if we consider the role that the denial of the father's agency played in the transition from patriarchy, as a modified omnipotent claim, to the rampant omnipotence of modernity ruled by capitalism. While a patriarchal culture formally denies the mother, it stops short of denying any indebtedness at all. It of course accords considerable recognition to the father's creative agency. The point at which a patriarchal culture in the West began to give way to a liberal-democratic one marks the birth of real modernity. It is the point at which the power and claims made in the name of fathers began to be limited, in favour of 'individuals' without a past, without an origin.

It is also the point, as we have seen, where the notion that individuals are contained systems, in energetic terms, comes into being.

This transitional point deserves attention. Liberalism cloaks the desires in the foundational fantasy with a more acceptable vocabulary, a vocabulary that is confusing, because it amalgamates foundational thinking with the appeal to tolerance. And this appeal, together with the injunctions to *judge not*, to do unto others as you would be done by, constitutes the most enduring opposition to the projected aggression that lies at the heart of the foundational fantasy. But while the earliest vocabulary of liberalism embodies this amalgam, it also recognizes dominion. It stakes out territory free of fathers and God slowly, and often reluctantly. Thus the foremost exponent of the origins of liberalism, John Locke, was himself 'for a fleeting moment'[12] caught in the tensions between the absence of God as a possibility and the requirements of Locke's own Christianity.

> A dependent intelligent being is under the power and direction and dominion of him on whom he depends and must be for the ends appointed him by the superior being. If man were independent he could have no law but his own will, no end but himself. He would be a god to himself.[13]

Dunn, after quoting this passage, goes on to add that 'when God in due course died, man, an intelligent being, no longer aware of any other being on whom he *was* dependent, set himself to try to be [a god]'.[14] And there we have it precisely. As long as the vocabulary of dependence, dominion and direction was retained, the implications of an egoistic liberalism were not spelt out.[15] At the same time, the insistence on that vocabulary points to the opposite possibility: a being without ties, dependent on no-one. In the logic of denial, then, the first step in the denial of God is the denial of the mother's agency, the second the denial of the father's. However, the denial of the mother's agency was no simple step. The Protestant's rejection of the Virgin's status buried an acknowledgement of the maternal that had compensated somewhat for other forms of denying the feminine. In the feudal times before the wholesale dominance of subject/object thought, Mary had even been associated with logic.[16]

Nor was the denial of the father's agency straightforward. God took time in dying, and the liberal rejection of dependence was aimed initially at the indebtedness presupposed in the patriarchal, feudal social contract. Pateman's argument that the social contract of Hobbes and Locke was essentially a fraternal contract is based on the idea that liberalism, in its origins, denied its dependence on the father in favour of a post-patriarchal orientation of man towards his equal brothers.[17] MacCannell's wonderful study shows how the 'regime of the brother'[18] ushers in the death of God and superego, together with a sexist system of power without accountability. The individual brothers answer to no-one. By the twentieth century, man had become 'a prosthetic God'.[19] His technology abets his deification, as did the discovery that his origin was a Mendelian accident. The puzzling popularity Darwin enjoyed in his own times[20] ceases to be problematic if it is situated on a continuum of increasing narcissism. So situated, Darwinism represents a confirmation of the idea that we humans are the most intelligent beings existing, not in God's image, but accordingly without peer.

It must be said that part of the problem here lies in the notion of 'God's image'. The term 'image' suggests something that can be represented two-dimensionally, and it is an easy slide from there to anthropomorphism. I would not object to God being known as the Good, if the term was not restricted to the idea of human virtue. Rather, the Good would be the Good ruling the laws of life, so that this term would connote an endless fullness of living energy, capacities, and above all an intelligence, beyond our own.

Not that human intelligence is inconsiderable. As a species joined in opposing lines over the fallen angel of death – a perverse source of light or brilliance – human beings may reacquire that brilliance by struggling to redirect it towards the right end. This is implicit in the notion that as one resists the blandishments of narcissistic fantasy, there is more energy available for the business of thinking, and acting. As the next chapter will suggest in more detail, as and if one acts against the foundational fantasy within and without, it fades in its force. This action is the human responsibility attached to the faculties of will and judgement. It is not for the Good to play the part of a stern and unrelenting paternal judge, striking down those who make the mess. Cleaning up a mess, as with all housework, is the responsibility of those who have made it. The question, really, is whether the Good would go against its nature by striking down any living thing, even those who do evil. But I should immediately qualify this question and recall that the laws of life ultimately constrain all the effects of evil; by these laws, even death can be made to do good in the end.

The problem remains that human intelligence, dulled by the increasing deadness of modernity's energetics, believes more and more in its claim to be the most superior of intelligences. Well before Darwin was popular, man's politics, and his related if anterior endorsement of a distinct, *interior* identity anticipate this claim. The abolition of any mediation between man and God takes us that much closer to the godhead craved. 'Capitalism' and its technology is evidently not the sole cause of man's newfound godhead, but the process of capitalization is critical to the physical alterations which make atheism less of an intellectual decision than a position based on emotional resistance to its alternative.[21] For myself, stepping for a moment into the benighted genre of personal criticism, my intellectual convictions here conflict with a resistance to the idea of an easy way out, and I suppose this is standard.

But on the continuum of increasing narcissism feudal patriarchy remains a mid-way step, between what the fantasy denies and what it seeks to accomplish. Yet this is no uninterrupted continuum. It is riddled with discontinuities. A close study of these discontinuities would, I think, show something very important about the question of scale. Part of the problem with the disputes over whether economic shifts preceded ideological shifts in the rise of capitalism is the relative neglect of scale. We have seen that usury abetted the accumulation of capital from the 12th century. There were pockets of small-scale capital within the larger scale feudal economy. We are aware that demands for liberty, individual rights and individual conscience (the Protestant ethic)[22] were articulated before capital becomes the dominant economy. If we take account of scale, we may at some future point be able to trace a dialectic between small-scale shifts to capitalization, and an increase in the articulation of subject-centred demands, where the symbolization of the demands in turn enforces the power of capital.

Overall, scale is obviously critical in my argument, which is built on interpreting the relation between microcosmic and macrocosmic versions, or perceptions, of an identical phenomenon. It is also built on the idea that the extent to which the foundational fantasy takes hold subjectively or psychically depends on the extent to which it is materially acted out. Thus the burden of this analysis is that attempts at symbolizing alternatives to the fantasy in the present will fail without alterations in economic scale, because the monetary economic dimension is the key to the fantasy's global dominance – its *increasing* materialization (it is always material).

Any increase in materialization depends on the fantasy's symbolization at some level, even if the level is only that of articulated subjective desire. Moreover, in discussing the foundational fantasy's universality in the past, we are only able to refer to its symbolization. I do not dispute this limitation. But this limitation, the limitation imposed by the inscribed record, means that symbolization itself is sometimes taken as the sole cure for present ills. This of course I do dispute, because it discounts the interaction between symbolization and scale, and the complexities of what should not be symbolized, as well as what should.[23] Skinner makes the point that the available vocabularies of agents and the meaning they have act as a constraint on their action,[24] but this works both ways. We need a vocabulary which constrains manifestations of a destructive psychical fantasy, as well as one that symbolizes the relation to maternal origin.

For, of itself, this symbolization does nothing to oppose certain elements of the fantasy (the objectification of the other by means ranging from devouring to dismembering, the denial of agency and conation in matter, the omnipotent control that would have it come to you without delay): elements which, when acted out on larger scales, result in a world in which more and more occupy the psychical and economic position of objects, reinforcing the crazed whims of an unseen subject, whose position they or we aspire to even against our judgement.

In the world of objects, the historical discontinuities, the breaks in scale and symbolisation, are overridden more and more by an homogenizing force, in which both scale and the cultures manifesting the fantasy reinforce one another. We now exist in a world in which the desires of the fantasy have ever more licence, in terms of the appropriation and control of human and natural energy. What is also clear is that while an articulation of demands based on these desires could and still does erupt in small locales, those demands are now becoming global. This is a necessary consequence of acting out the fantasy with ever-larger precision, because this extends the physical grip of the fantasy on individual persons. It remains to see just how it comes about.

Our argument here will depend on analysing how history is constructed as a *material* narrative. In turn, this depends on analysing the slower time and wider space over which the ego's era is played out, thereby completing the account of how the fantasy is enacted on a scale with an ever-enlarging compass, and how techno-economic dynamics reinforce the desires in the fantasy at the expense of other psychical possibilities. In other words, this reinforcement alters the *physis* in ways which make it harder to act if not think outside foundational terms, precisely because of the energetic changes they effect.

The key to the alterations in the *physis* lie in the terms time and space. Time and space are basic to the dynamics whereby the foundational fantasy is generated. We want it now, and we want it to come to us. On the social scale, by inventing technologies that bring whatever it is we want to us, and which do so immediately, we are abolishing time. But, paradoxically, as we have seen, this entails extending the fantasy in space and, for a reason yet to be determined, giving it more time to play itself out: instead of a lifetime, or the years of an individual psychosis, this spans a few centuries. The only way of resolving this paradox, and the tautology that this argument becomes without that resolution, is to suppose that as we extend the fantasy in space, and make it immediately present, we simultaneously slow down time. In turn, this means supposing that the mechanism by which we make the fantasy present and extend its spatial coverage also congeals or slows down time. What is this mechanism, and how is the paradox to be resolved?

I have established that the paradox is resolved in the case of infancy and the birth of psychical reality in this way: what prompts the hallucination is the desire that the longed-for object be present here and now. Hallucination not only introduces instant gratification (in theory); in practice, it also introduces delay. In the social case, technology constructs the commodities that satisfy the fantasy of instant gratification and service, but how do these constructions simultaneously slow things down, especially as production is getting faster and faster? The key here was the notion that the ego's own hallucinated responses constitute the first point of resistance. We supposed that the construction of a commodity also binds energy in the same way that it is bound in the repression of a hallucination. In both cases the energy is attached to an image, fixing it in place. The commodity, like the hallucination, constitutes a point of resistance, in that it encapsulates living nature in forms which remove them from the flow of life, just as the repressed hallucination traps psychical energy in a constructed self-contained boundary that founds the subject. In other words, the fixed points of commodities function analogously with hallucinations and fantasies in that they bind living substances in forms which are inert, relative to the energetic movement of life.

The labour theory of value without the subject/object distinction shows how these fixed points must accumulate ever more rapidly, relative to the movement of life, which has to be cheated on, in order to make a profit. The more of these relatively inert points there are – and they are of course more significant, more fixed, when the commodity produced is not biodegradable – the slower the movement of life becomes. Thus the notion that points of resistance slow things down provides a critical principle by which to gauge what should and should not be constructed. That gauge is: how readily can these constructions re-enter the movement of life?

The notion that points of resistance slow things down also means we can account for the paradox whereby the fantasy takes more time to play itself out historically (more time than it does in individual human life), in a way consistent with the idea that the fantasy simultaneously extends itself in space. It takes more 'time' to play itself out in the sense that it uses more living energy, as it systematically extends itself in the spatial conquests necessary to supply the living substances by which it sustains itself. However, it also follows from this argument that the 'time' it takes to play itself out is itself a constructed phenomenon, in that this 'time' consists of the accumulation of 'points of resistance' or commodities. Moreover this 'time' has its own direction.

The construction of one commodity (using the term in the broadest sense)[25] fixes a relatively inert or still point. This point (let us say it is a factory, even a town) then functions as an inert point of reference from which distances are measured and pathways built. They are built, at least in part, as a means to further the consumption of more living substances in the process of production. Of the different characteristics that mark the networks established by these means, there are two that need to be recalled here. The first is that, to stay in the race of efficient consumption for production and further consumption, these networks need to facilitate the most rapid transport of energy possible. This applies to energy of any order: the natural substances consumed in production, and human labour-power. The means by which natural substance or labour is extracted and conveyed from A to B has to be speeded up. This is why, at the level of constructed space–time, everything seems to be getting faster and faster. The second point about the networks constructed in relation to still points is that at the same time as they partake in the process whereby natural reproduction is actually slowed down, they must, like the still points themselves, have their own physical energetic effects. These effects are also physical in the sense that commodities function as points of resistance to natural rhythms, so that in reality, things get slower and slower.

As the networks between these points extend, creating more still points in the process, the expanding spatio-temporal construction that results has a pattern of its own. There is every reason for supposing that this pattern presents itself to us as temporal causality.[26] Temporal causality is the process whereby one thing appears to lead to another across time in an apparently irreversible manner. This taken-for-granted process is of course at issue in physics, where the asymmetrical nature of time, the puzzle as to why time only goes one way, or why time is irreversible, is regarded as something to be explained. By this account, time could be understood, in theory if not in practice, as reversible, provided that all the points of resistance out of which space–time is constructed and connected were systematically undone, and if their component natural substances re-entered the natural rhythms of production, from which they were initially, physically, 'abstracted'. This understanding of time also accords with the deconstructionist idea that causality is a construction, a line of reasoning we impose on events, except that, by my argument, the causal construction really has been constructed. The fact that the construction has a fantasmatic origin makes it no less physical in its effects. In other words, to read causality as a mere illusion, which could be done away with by refusing to impose causal reasoning in theory, accords with and therefore does nothing to counter the galloping construction of causality in the physical world. By the same token, to read narrative as a mistaken imposition of a linear discourse on a situation whose polymorphous facticity will not brook it, is to overlook the extent to which a narrative line has been produced as a physical, material reality. That narrative owes its existence to a process in which the desires of the fallen have shifted from the transient realm of individual psychical life to become dominant across time, but the present effects of that process are such as to make it difficult to trace the narrative.

The reader may have noted that, apart from detailing the myth of the Fall, I have resisted the question as to whether the origin of the fantasy is individual or social. Certainly knowledge of the fantasy is an individual, psychical matter. But the fact that knowledge was first gained at this individual psychical location does not, necessarily, make the individual psyche the fantasy's origin as such. Indeed the arguments about the transmission of energy and affect, and the illusion of self-containment, together with those on the conventional but illogical nature of the distinction between mind and body, ideas and matter, make the idea of an individual origin problematic. Moreover, it is only possible to write of a fantasy becoming material, of a material illusion, if ideas and matter are not opposed categories, but variations in physical density, for want of another term. A spoken idea, for instance, involves the energy of sound waves; a commodity the bound energy of matter. What makes a fantasy fantasmatic is not that it lacks matter or energy. It is rather that it is absurd, lacking reality. As Hegel had it: 'all that is real is rational, and all that is rational is real'.

If there is a common origin, outside the psyche or the social, the most obvious culprit is inertia and the binding of energy in fixed points, whether in the psyche or in the form of money and commodities. The birth of the fixed point generates a chain reaction: without it, there is no comparison; without comparison there is neither pride nor envy. But if inertia is the original culprit, this would mean that the Fall of the angels should be interpreted as the birth of inertia, a kind of cosmic accident, something we do not yet know or understand, but towards whose explanation the findings of physics may tend ultimately. Whether a cosmic accident – in which what was hitherto freely mobile became fixed – could explain the negative affects themselves, (envy, greed, aggression and so forth) is another matter. But given that ideas and matter are only split 'after the Fall', then we might suppose that justice, mercy, love, above all life itself, are inherent to that free energy, just as objectification, domination, control and death inhere in the fixity opposed to that energy. But if we entertain this thought, the question must become: how did a cosmic accident lodge itself in the minds and psyche of a western and white world? Is the fact that Lucifer is the angel of deceptive vision, while hallucination gets the infantile fantasy underway, significant? Until and if a hypothesis sufficient to those questions can be formulated, I will proceed on the assumption that human beings, through the experience of delay, hallucination and fixity are born with a kind of original sin (I return to that issue in the next chapter). I will also continue to assume that the fantasy as an individual affair is reinforced both by the fact that energetic affects are not self-contained, and because the dynamics of inertia and fixity in the historical realm of commodification must be cumulative.

The dynamics described in this process must be cumulative, not only in the sense that, as things move faster and faster at the level of constructed space–time, they become slower and slower in relation to the natural logic they attempt to rival. The dynamics must also be cumulative in terms of the extent to which the causality constructed presents itself to us as a historical process.

'History', as the sense of the sequence of past events, is increasingly moulded by the extent to which a foundational fantasy makes itself materially true, and by its consequent material effects on the individual psyches that entertain the fantasy, effects that are experienced and compounded by the transmission of affect. This is why grasping the fact that the fantasy has become a material narrative across time is so critical, if so difficult. It is critical in creating a monolithic view of history which has a material basis in the present, but which had to cover over all sorts of local differences to attain supremacy. Even so, these differences still erupt, in uncovering what the written record has not included hitherto. In this respect, reflection and research, as the uncovering and correcting of what has been omitted or distorted, are always anti-foundational.

As we have seen, the materialization of the narrative is also critical in creating, and then undermining, the historical sense as such. The postmodern oblivion to, if not its condemnation of, history has a predecessor. 'Thinking historically' has not always been with us, only to be abandoned in the present. At first glance, it seems that it is only as the shifts in social organization become sufficiently marked as to be memorable within an individual lifetime that the historical sense is born. The problem with this is that dramatic changes had occurred within the span of individual lifetimes hitherto: had I been born in France in the thirteenth century, been a mercenary or a saint or even a literate priest, I would have witnessed the departure of one king, the reinstatement of another, etc. On the other hand, one could reply that such shifts in social organization were not sufficiently widereaching or fundamental in their effects as to have brought a historical consciousness into being. Yet this only mitigates the objection that changes occurred in individual lifetimes beforehand. It does not resolve it. One can only explain why rapid shifts infiltrate consciousness and intellectual awareness with more power, why the sense of stasis declines in and especially after the seventeenth century – although that static sense had survived major historical alterations hitherto – if the power of the historical sense is understood literally, as a physical force. It can be understood in this way if the shifts in social organization result in a sense of the passage of time that propels one to locate events and experience in time and space. Yet what would such a sense involve? It would have to have two ingredients. Any sense of time has to be based on a feeling of motion. To feel motion, one has to have a fixed reference point, fixed relative to one's motion (or one can be that fixed point, and feel the other's motion). The second ingredient is that this feeling of motion has to be sufficiently rapid to mean that there is a need to locate events and experience. And these can only be located in fixed points of reference. In other words, the historical sense requires not only motion, but fixed points that do not change. From this perspective, it seems that where energy boundaries and technology are concerned, we are dealing with something like a three-stage process historically. The first stage is charted in the pre-Renaissance writings discussed in Part I; the second stage is embodied in the notion of a self-contained, interiorized consciousness; the third is the return of the repressed, the idea of energetic connection. In other words, the notion of the self-contained individual marks an interregnum, which is also characterized by interiorized thinking and historical consciousness.[27]

Yet the technological correspondences of these stages break down, in that the first stage refers to a less technological or built in environment; the third, which is apparently similar to it, to a highly technologized context. However, this similarity can be explained to the extent that both the technologized and untechnologized environments affect the sense of history and passing time. The untechnologized environment has been correlated with stasis, with the sense of no change: in this sense it is opposed to a historical consciousness. The highly technologized environment has been correlated with change that is so rapid that it also has negative effects on historical perception. However, if I am right, while this environment militates against a sense of history, it should none the less be one in which there is a sense that there is never 'enough time'. I am presuming that all these effects are energetic, and that they impinge on perception not just because of their content, but because they also impinge on the boundaries by which the subject maintained its material illusion of containment.

Both the first and third stage are marked not only by the ideas of connection and transmission, but by perceptions which would now be styled paranoid. In the contemporary West, any perception of an ideational force on the subject that comes from without is liable to be designated this way. But it will be designated this way, in part, because it conflicts with the inherited and hegemonic symbolic. Thus one of the things this analysis points to is the importance of symbolizing the notion of interconnecting forces, and thus understanding their material effects.

If these material effects are taken into account, the extent to which the fantasy takes hold individually, and thus the extent to which individuals act in accord with the fantasy's constructed causal direction, should be cumulative. What I want to suggest now is that just as its own fantasies weigh heavily upon the ego, so does a subjective if subliminal sensing of what is animate or inanimate in the surrounding environment. The less animate that environment is and the slower time becomes in natural reality, the greater the ego's need to speed things up, its anxiety, its splitting, its need for control, its 'cutting up' in its urge to know, its spoiling of living nature, and its general aggression towards the other. But of course, as with any paranoid anxiety, the ego by these processes only accelerates the production of the conditions that produce its fears.[28] It constructs more fixed points which start, or speed up, the whole show again. At the same time, it uproots itself and its anchors in the interpersonal fixed points (or enduring relationships) which defined it hitherto, which also short-circuits its memory. And by this very uprooting, it breaks down the identity barriers which preserved some form of individuality, leading to psychotic anxieties, and increasing the exhaustion of the modern subject. The anxiety generated by this process is exacerbated by the failure to symbolise energetic connections, connections which are experienced through the ego's lens, assimilated to a subject-centred worldview. Thus they are experienced fleetingly, as displacement removes the anchors which barred knowledge of them. The failure to find a vocabulary of connections, to symbolize them in terms which are not subject-centered, means that any feeling of connection will only be experienced through the ego's lens, assimilated to a subject-centred world view. This is the essence of a major symptom of paranoid anxiety: the awareness of energetic forces in the environment (an accurate awareness), accompanied by the belief that these forces are focussed solely on one's individual self (not an accurate belief).

Other symptoms of this process are evident in how symbolized ethical codes break down to accommodate an increasing incapacity to tolerate delay, a greater demand for service, a more extensive need for domination, a horror of inferiority contingent on escalating envy and the constant comparisons envy demands. These things are accommodated, but within vocabularies or codes of symbolization which are more concerned with flattery than courtesy, ranging from subject-positioning encounters in the everyday ('Yes sir, right away sir, did you enjoy your meal?') to judicious quotation. In writing, they are reflected in a rhythmless prose, bearing the marks of dead fixed points. In theory, they are also reflected in an ever-rising flight away from the concrete and the flesh into the fantasmatic world of the abstract. It is this last flight that makes the sometimes obvious nature of the processes recorded here elusive.

The originating foundational fantasy situates the mother as a passive natural entity responding to an active agency located elsewhere, but this is becoming, or has become, more than an ephemeral fantasy. The extent to which active agency really is located elsewhere increases as the material means to control the environment increase, as they do when the fantasy is acted out. To the extent that this active agency results in the imposition of a direction on the environment which goes against, rather than with, natural rhythms and their own logic, the force of the latter figures less in any calculations made about what causes what, especially in the realms of social theory. At the same time, the active agency, the will at issue, is reduced too readily to individual actions. In fact the location of this agency is problematic in the extreme. A direction which goes against natural logic and rhythms is imposed, but while individuals strive for the subject position, it eludes them. They are constituted as objects unable to sustain a direction of their own, who labour under perceptions which reinforce their strivings for the subject position, while affecting their perception in ways which make it difficult to analyse the basis of the strivings.

By this argument, the subject's sense of connection with the world is physically altered by its physical environment.

And if the physical points of resistance embodied in commodities function after the manner of fantasies, closing the
subject off to the movement of life, they are also visual tan-
gible evidence of a different physical world which, however
fantasmatic its origin, makes the subject more likely to see
what it has made, rather than feel itself to be connected
with, or part of, what has made it.[29] This constitutes the
main limitation on any wholesale endorsement of Spinoza's
theory. The equation of God and Nature is limited by the fact
that nature is perceived, from a human subject-centred
standpoint, in terms of visual and tactile extension. Spinoza
himself noted the limitation, in so far as he noted that while
the One Substance had infinite attributes, humans perceived
only two: extension and thought. But, for this very reason,
there is always a 'beyond' to what we perceive. My point
here is that while this 'beyond' is never immaterial, while it
is always physical in some sense, it cannot be limited to
'nature' as we perceive it. Thomas Aquinas's parallel point
is that nature does in restricted terms what God does in
unrestricted terms. Yet if Nature is restricted in my argument, it is restricted even more as we progressively make
our restricting, subject-centred perspective of the world
more concrete. For in modernity the visual hallucination
which denied feelings of unpleasure is now a concrete thing,
and the various senses which otherwise connect the subject
with the world stand back in favour of the visual sense.

The idea that the subject's sense of perception is physically
altered by its physical environment, and the related idea that
the concrete imposition of a foundational psychical fantasy
has altered that environment, raise the possibility that
different physical theories and theories of perception are
more true for their times than they appear with hindsight,
precisely because the times physically alter what and how we
perceive. The subject-centered world view literally changed
the sense of perspective in the early Renaissance, when
perspective was delineated from the viewer's standpoint.
The Medievalists literally saw things differently.[30] Nor was
artistic perspective the only thing to shift. Related to that
shift, and, according to Conley, a possible precursor of it,

was the urge to map the world from the subject's standpoint. For Conley the preoccupation with mapping was a condition of the emergence of 'selfhood and self-fashioning'.[31] Moving closer to present time: Žižek suggests that it is 'probably more than a coincidence that . . . the theory of relativity paved the way for a notion of the universe as a time-space continuum, i.e., for a 'static' picture of the universe where time is conceived as the fourth dimension of space'. The theory of relativity, for him, has to be located in a context where temporality has been displaced in favour of spatiality.[32]

If the parallel drawn here between psychical and socio-historical temporal dynamics is correct, if the construction of more and more commodities slows down real time while seeming to speed it up, then this means the physical reality in which we exist, the physical laws under which we live, *are being and have been altered*. From this perspective, the idea, common from the Bhagavad Gita to Nietzsche, that human history is organized into cycles which we are doomed to repeat, may be explained in terms of every civilization passing a critical point at which it has bound more and more life and living energy in forms which cannot reproduce themselves. Binding more and more energy upsets the balance of nature, unless we unbind, which means retracing our economic (though not our patriarchal) steps. But we could of course retrace those economic steps. We are not doomed to repeat. We can judge modernity as that process which needs to be reversed here and now. Critical in this reversal is the acknowledgement of the mother, whose denial begins a socio-historical process which binds energy past the point where existing life in all its species can be sustained. The question becomes: does that denial and the deathly process that results from it upset the physical balance as well as the biological one? By a socio-historical process, have we contributed to the chaotic *physis* we now discover, the uncertainty remarked upon now,[33] as if it had always been present? For if we have, we have done so by enacting a fantasy which, because it relies on a divorce of mental and physical activity, reinforces the prejudice that a socio-historical process has no effect on the physical world; this prejudice in thought may be why it is difficult to get clear information from a scientist to the question just posed.

But while different theories of physics and the natural order may have more relevance for their times than they appear to have from the present standpoint, retrospectives on paths to the present, theories of social and historical change, will be limited by the blindspots of the present. Marxism partially explained the process involved, and this was the immense appeal of this most successful of master-narratives. It failed as a narrative not because it was a narrative, but because it began the story in the wrong place, and left something vital out. It left out the fact that 'materialism', meaning the quite literal concretization of the fantasy, its physical enactment with its physical effects, has increasingly made itself into a determinant reality, a reality that overrides that of nature.

Had it been a theory of how the economic is increasingly determinant of the character of this epoch, Marxism may have extended its explanatory reach. Socialism, as a pro-grammatic solution to the ills of capitalism, misses because it half counters the fantasy we have analysed without fully knowing why. It remained bound by the gigantic scale the old system of production demands. In part, this was because in attempting to mark out what makes labour distinct from nature, Marx ran together the ability to imagine and design with the ability to create value. To say the same thing, he ran together the general properties of labour across time with the specific properties of productive labour under capital. At the same time, Marx's theory shows how subjective capacities, themselves appropriated in the first instance, are then reappropriated or alienated by capital, and removed from the new class of human objects. They are appropriated in the first instance in that it is the fantasmatic belief that it is the source of agency and direction that brings the subject into being. The labour process under capital replays the dynamics of this appropriation in every detail where nature is concerned, and the extent to which it replays it with people positions them in class terms, and/or in terms of exploitation.

In this argument so far we have foreshadowed that the nature of exploitation takes place at two levels: the energetic, interpersonal level and the economic level. In the next chapter, I will try to show how these levels are related. We will see that the twisted potential of this dual exploitation has not yet been exhausted, even though the beings who endure it are rapidly becoming exhausted themselves, both by the energy they turn back against themselves and by the environmental debris they have to negotiate. An earth and a people whose vital variety is dulled in this way, and dulled further by the deaths of more and more species whose diversity once enhanced our own, an earth where breathing gets harder as the air gets hotter, is rather like hell. Indeed, where else is hell but on earth, here and soon? I hinted earlier that more than a parallel between a theological myth and the trajectory of modernity was at stake. A time, after Einstein, is always a place seen from somewhere else. If hell is this place here on earth and soon, then, in the ever-changing perspectives of other spaces, it is also an eternal time. We Luciferian humans seem to be succeeding in our ambition of building 'hell as a rival to heaven'. While that hell cannot last long on earth, it will last forever (as hell is meant to do) in the endless perturbations of perception.

Notes

1 Lacan, 'The Function and Field of Speech and Language in Psycho analysis' (The Rome Report) [1953], in *Écrits: A Selection*, pp. 30–113.
2 Christopher Lasch, *The Culture of Narcissism: American Life in an Age of Diminishing Expectations* (New York: Norton, 1978).
3 Jürgen Habermas, *Knowledge and Human Interests* [1968], tr. Jeremy J. Shapiro (Boston: Beacon Press, 1971).
4 Nancy Fraser's critique of Habermas makes the inherently patriarchal longing at base of his lament very clear. Nancy Fraser, *Unruly Practices: Power, Discourse and Gender in Contemporary Social Theory* (Cambridge: Polity Press, 1990).
5 On this point see Joan Copjec's 'Vampires, Breast-Feeding and Anxiety', in *Read My Desire: Lacan Against the Historicists* (Cambridge, MA: MIT Press, 1994).
6 The Gnostic gospel of Phillip shows that it was commonplace to

see the third element of the divine being as female. The esoteric Phillip is ridiculing those who take the Virgin Birth literally. 'Some said, "Mary conceived by the holy spirit." They are in error. They do not know what they are saying; for when did a female ever conceive by a female?' Quoted in Elaine Pagels, *The Origin of Satan* (New York: Vintage Books, 1995), p. 175.

7 At the outset we perceived that conflict in Lucifer's desire to build hell as a rival to heaven. The desire to reverse positions, to put the mother in the place of the dependent child, was there paralleled in Lucifer's desire to be boss.

8 A probably obvious aside. Many of the desires which seem universal register their universality culturally, not in terms of individual behaviour. Thus if one thinks of the psychical permutations of devouring, one might think of Thyestes being served his son at dinner, not of Ancient Greeks sitting down to filial meals as a matter of course. Whether the power of various myths can be attributed to the unconscious chords they touch, or whether they should be seen in terms of an intersubjective unconscious which may or may not register in separate persons, does not matter to the extent that, in both cases, the social nature of the foundational fantasy is confirmed, although the choice of options would influence the causal weight given to the social manifestation.

9 There is a small anthropological literature, and some historical discussion, of children's play. The main difficulty with evaluating the anthropological material is the extent to which children are conceived and conceive of themselves as children, or alternatively as small people. Cf. Philippe Ariès, *Centuries of Childhood: A Social History of Family Life*, tr. Robert Baldick (New York: Vintage Books, 1962); and Michel Foucault, *The Archaeology of Knowledge and the Discourse on Language* [1969], tr. A. M. Sheridan Smith (New York: Harper, 1976).

10 While I suspect the fantasized attacks on and denigration of the mother's body are universal, I do not want to claim that they are universal without the monumental cross-cultural research that would need to be done to substantiate the claim. However, one immediately thinks of the anthropological line of enquiry extending from Margaret Mead, *Male and Female: A Study of the Sexes in a Changing World* (New York: William Morrow, 1950), through to, for example, researchers such as Gillian Gillison, 'Images of Nature in Gimi Thought' in M. Strathern and C. MacCormack (eds.), *Nature, Culture and Gender* (Cambridge: Cambridge University Press, 1980), pp. 143–73. Gillison's research on the Gimi in Papua New Guinea lends itself well to

the psychoanalytic interpretation she gives it. During male initiation rites, flutes, which Gillison describes as 'symbolic penes' are shown to the boys, and (a secret kept from the women) the boys are informed that '"in truth, it was once something that belonged only to women. It wasn't ours! We men stole it!"' Ibid., p. 156. See also Gillison's *Between Culture and Fantasy: A New Guinea Highlands Mythology* (Chicago: University of Chicago Press, 1993).

11 Val Plumwood, *Feminism and the Mastery of Nature* (London and New York: Routledge, 1993).

12 John Dunn, *Western Political Theory in the Face of the Future* (Cambridge: Cambridge University Press, 1978), p. 40.

13 Ibid.

14 Ibid.; see also John Dunn, *The Political Thought of John Locke; An Historical Account of the 'Two Treatises of Government'* (Cambridge: Cambridge University Press, 1969).

15 Dunn's broader thesis, that it was possible for Locke to think as he did *because* he was a Christian does not, of course, abolish the fact that Locke thought as he did.

16 Richard W. Southern, *The Making of the Middle Ages* (London: Cresset Library, 1953).

17 Carole Pateman, *The Sexual Contract* (Cambridge: Polity, 1988).

18 Juliet F. MacCannell, *The Regime of the Brother: After the Patriarchy* (London and New York: Routledge, 1991).

19 Freud, *Civilization and its Discontents* [1929], *SE*, vol. 21.

20 Richard Rorty, 'Anti-Foundationalism and Sentimentality', paper presented at Cambridge Political Thought Seminar, March 1993.

21 While the concern with the psychical origins of atheism is not of particular interest to them, the question of divinity and more generally spirituality is returning in some of the feminist writing I have already mentioned. Both Kristeva and Irigaray see some form of divine representation of the 'feminine' as critical to counteracting the worst effects of patriarchy and the patriarchal social contract. Thus Kristeva sees the Virgin Mary as a figurative check on the 'powers of horror', while Irigaray sees a symbolic feminine Godhead as a means of guaranteeing woman's origin and thence identity. See Julia Kristeva, *Tales of Love* [1983], tr. Leon S. Roudiez (New York: Columbia University Press, 1987), pp. 374 ff.; and Luce Irigaray, 'Divine Women', tr. Stephen Muecke, *Local Consumption* (Sydney Occasional Paper no. 9, 1986). The difficulty with these writings is less with the writings as such than with the commentators' attempts to deal with the embarrassment of having an otherwise admired

thinker apparently endorsing God. Both Margaret Whitford, *Luce Irigaray: Philosophy in the Feminine* (London and New York: Routledge, 1990), and E. A. Grosz, 'Irigaray and the Divine', *Local Consumption* (Sydney Occasional Paper no. 9, 1986), for whose deployments of Irigaray I have the greatest respect, conclude that Irigaray is not so much a believer as a strategist. Her appeal to the divine is read as a 'strategy' for undermining the existing symbolic, as well as a means for women counteracting the death drive through faith in female and feminine worth and goodness. The problem with seeing the advocacy of faith in a maternal or feminine divinity as a strategy is that one has to ask the question: strategy for whom? If 'we' (academics?) know that God does not exist but 'they' need to believe that she does, what precisely are we saying? And if we see it as a strategy, from where will we derive the power of conviction in our own female worth which would protect us from the death drive, to which we are also liable? In this context, note too that Irigaray is also conscious of spirituality and divinity in terms of the fact that ideas have been split from 'matter'. 'Our so-called human theories and our most banal discourses are moving away from these things, progressing through and with a language which forgets the matter it designates and through which it speaks.' Irigaray, 'Divine Women', p. 1. I could not agree more with these sentiments, as the above should make evident.

22 Quentin Skinner, *The Foundations of Modern Political Thought* (2 vols) (Cambridge: Cambridge University Press, 1978), vol. I, p. 1.

23 Cf. Quentin Skinner, *Meaning and Context: Quentin Skinner and his Critics*, ed. James Tully (Cambridge: Polity Press, 1988), p. 132.

24 Ibid.

25 A commodity varies in scale depending on the position of the consumer. From the standpoint of one consumer, it could be a small-scale consumer good. From the standpoint of another, it could be a major chemical multinational such as ICI.

26 Drucilla Cornell, *The Philosophy of the Limit* (New York and London: Routledge, 1992), whose comments on temporal causality are developed in the context of a critique of Niklas Luhmann. Luhmann recognizes the Parsonian point that a temporal social system can only be compared to something that is not temporal. Niklas Luhmann, *The Differentiation of Society* [1975], tr. Stephen Holmes and Charles Larmore (New York: Columbia University Press, 1982), p. 292. He even says that it can only be

compared to something that is 'immediate', that is to say, time-less. But having had this insight, he then goes on to neglect its implications altogether. He forgets the existence of the 'immediate' something, and argues instead that a temporal system can have nothing outside itself, and thus that there is no point against which an alternative future to the one already contained within the present can be built. From the perspective of this argument, of course, that alternative point is present in the natural world. Moreover, as I imply in the text, if the 'immediate' something is the physical world, if the physical world is also spatio-temporal, from whence does it get its temporality, if not from the social world? Cornell criticizes Luhmann's 'privileging of the present' from a Derridean perspective. Cornell, *The Philosophy of the Limit*. The significance of time and space in social organizations generally, and the shift from modernism to 'postmodernism' in particular, is the central theme of Anthony Giddens, *The Consequences of Modernity* (Stanford: Stanford University Press, 1990).

27 Thinking historically appears to gather steam with the social changes that predate and accompany technological shifts. For instance, it is only in the late sixteenth century that the first histories, as the description of particular periods, begin to be written. Roberto Weiss, 'Scholarship from Petrarch to Erasmus', in D. Hay (ed.), *The Age of the Renaissance* (New York: McGraw-Hill, 1967), pp. 119–44. The classic distinction between cold and hot societies is a distinction between hot societies which have internalized their historicity, and cold ones which remain timeless. Claude Lévi-Strauss, *Structural Anthropology*, tr. C. Jacobson and B. G. Schoepf (New York: Basic Books, 1963). If Evans-Pritchard was right, a rise in historical consciousness requires (in effect) a memorable change in social structure and occasions for social mobility. It is when the social hierarchy is unchanged, when the same number of social places are available, that the 'distance between the beginning of the world and the present day seems unalterable'; Edward Evans-Pritchard, *The Nuer: A Description of the Modes of Livelihood and Political Institutions of a Nilotic People* (Oxford: Clarendon Press, 1940), p. 108.

28 There is a striking account of the paranoid's collusion in the production of the conditions it fears in Bersani's discussion of Thomas Pynchon. Leo Bersani, *The Culture of Redemption* (Cambridge, MA: Harvard University Press, 1990), p. 188.

29 Many feminist philosophers of science have suggested that the boundaries of the physical sciences and their underlying

assumptions should be thrown into question; there is no reason why the physical sciences should have escaped gender-blindness, when the social sciences have not. But there is a difference between noting that the physical sciences should be questioned, or even showing that a more empathetic approach to science is possible, and proposing an alternative, speculative, physical theory. This is not the exhortation. This is the act.

30 Teresa Brennan 'The Contexts of Vision' in *Vision and Context* Teresa Brennan and Martin Jay (eds) (New York and London: Routledge, 1996), pp. 217–28, p. 227.

31 Tom Conley, *The Self-Made Map: Cartographic Writing in Early Modern France* (Minneapolis: University of Minnesota Press, 1996), p. 6. Conley also reveals how the maternal, and sexual difference, 'everything that had seemed marginal to the enterprise of mapping the world, are . . . essential to it' (p. 309).

32 Slavoj Žižek, *Enjoy Your Symptom! Jacques Lacan in Hollywood and Out* (New York and London: Routledge, 1992), p. 64.

33 Werner Heisenberg, *Physics and Philosophy: The Revolution in Modern Science* (New York: Harper, 1958).

10

EXPLOITATION
AND OPPOSITION

By this book's argument, exploitation always involves an energetic transfer. In fact we can define exploitation on this basis: where there is no energetic transfer that depletes one agency while enriching the other, there is no exploitation. But exploitation in these terms does not only work at the economic level. It works at the interpersonal level as well, the level experienced in everyday personal and social life. In personal life, the wrong sex can assign one to a draining emotional tie, and an inexplicable fixity or inertia. In social interaction, this exploitation may be brief or glancing, but it is pervasive: the wrong accent, the wrong colour, the wrong sexuality can lead to a thousand slights in brief encounters, all of which give a temporary leverage to the subjects on the other side of them.

What I am terming interpersonal exploitation is not reducible to economic exploitation. But we can now see that these forms of exploitation are related. Interpersonal benefits accrue to the subject in the same way as economic benefits. In both cases, the one is empowered, subjectified, by the energy of the other. At the interpersonal level of image, and imaginary fixing, one 'makes it to subject' by directing aggression and a negative image outwards, freeing oneself to move. Such movement is enhanced by the attention directed towards the subject by the one who is fixed, seeking the affirmation that it is in the subject's energetic interest not to give. It is this 'attention', the intelligence, energy and direction it embodies, that is appropriated by the subject. At the economic level, the same capacities are appropriated to greater or lesser extents, and the extent to which they are appropriated is inversely proportionate, roughly speaking, to the wage. But they are appropriated, usually, on a different scale, and the subject who benefits is accordingly harder to locate; the object position, the position of the objectified other, is easier to identify.

Whilst the subject is harder to locate, we can make the subject and object positions the key terms in the dynamics of exploitation, and we can redefine the relation to exploitation in terms of the two levels they operate on. Those who occupy the object position in interpersonal and economic terms are doubly exploited. These are most likely to be women and ethnic and racial groups. But the *degree* of exploitation at either level also matters here, for exploitation at one level invariably shades into the other: a woman exploited in interpersonal life will find her economic power deteriorating, if for no other reason than that her confidence, her sense of her self as subject, is systematically eroded. The working-class man, denied the economic subject position, may find aggression giving way to prolonged depression. The aggression follows on from the fact that a person positioned as object economically will have a strong psychical drive to play subject in an interpersonal context. But the opportunities for discharging this drive are rarely sufficient to protect the part-time subject from depression, or to preempt it. Depression, if it is experienced only cyclically, or contextually, for an hour here or there, is another manifestation of the object position. This does not mean depression is always bad. It can be the moment at which the empowered subject becomes human, alert to the suffering of others. But I will leave for another place the question of how much gentler and kinder people are when their status as overweening subjects is in doubt. The point is that we are all of us at some moment objects, which will help explain why a privileged man may still experience himself as powerless and lacking. Yet such a subject will not be comparing himself to exploited others; he will be comparing himself to a super-Subject, some fictional character who receives more recognition and lives out the foundational fantasy's omnipotence more than he does himself. By 'democratic' standards, which make everything available to everyone in theory, we have all failed.

By whatever yardsticks, everyone then is positioned as subject and object in a variety of contexts. While the different levels of exploitation cannot be reduced to one another, their homology means we can define subject and object positions in terms of both economic and interpersonal recognition. Both make people rich or poor in a currency of empowering images and coins alike. Taking account of homologous levels of exploitation not only makes it plain why the object position is more likely to be occupied by the unwhite, the female, and the economically class-exploited; it also shows how it is occupied in a way which aligns its inhabitants with nature.

The alignment with nature is all the more crucial because, unless it is stressed, we will continue to want to be subjects. We want to be subjects even against our wills, because there is a politics of exhaustion being played out in relation to the fantasy on the global scale. We will want to be subjects to garner the energy needed to move – whether it is through the attentive recognition and labour of others, or those expensive 'labour-saving devices'. The consequence of living in the high-tech built environment is that one almost *has* to be a subject to repel its deadening effects. As I hope I have shown, these deadening effects are deceptive: the world from which they emanate appears to be a world of more rapid motion, with a rapid pulse that can for a time be taken as energy itself, as it speeds up one's conscious tempo. But the price of this temporary excitement will be paid somewhere. Even if it is not paid by the subject who benefits, the deadening effects of this environment more and more make each and everyone an object.

Still, as ever, the process of becoming either subject or object is complex, invariably overdetermined. The urge to resist objectification is very powerful, the life drive more enduring and effective than its fantasmatic parasite. I have indicated that resisting the object position can be done in

two ways: by striving for subjectivity through the exploitation of others, or seeking to release the life drive by other
means. But there is no immediate penalty for exploitation.
Exploiting subjects often thrive: they are 'by any ethological
standard of the bright eye and the gleaming coat, danger-
ously flourishing'.[1] Nor is there a guarantee that the
exploited will opt for a non-exploitative release; we are, for
example, now familiar enough with those flourishing female
subjects whose feminism goes all the way to the bank but no
further.

That aside: the relation between increasing objectification and the positioning of the white, masculine subject is
unclear. But it is clear the man is more likely to occupy the
object position as the burden of fixity produced by his environment increases, and as his traditional others become less
willing and less able to accept the object position, with the
burden of fixity it entails. At first I thought that this heavier
burden would lead to more objectification of the other by
those still clinging to the subject position, and that racism
and sexism would increase accordingly. I am now less sure,
and think there are two or three trends at work here.
Probably the objectification of the other by those clinging to
the subject position is increasing; but so are the counter-
projections of those aspiring to that position, and/or reject-
ing the object position by other means. In the relations
between women and men, there does seem to be an
increasing antagonism, escalating projections, and a level
of paranoia which makes trust difficult to sustain for more
than short bursts. While the paranoia in contemporary
sexual difference deserves more extended treatment, the
point here is that this paranoia is but a stage in an overall
objectifying process which targets everything living. As and
if this process becomes clearer, so will the fact that the
economy of the large scale is making a fiction of the subject
position. Aspire to it as they may, fewer and fewer attain it.

What then are the alternatives to that subjection, the means
for seeking release which do not replicate its dynamics? It is
clear that these alternatives would have to hold at the level
of interpersonal life, the realm of ethical decision, as well as

at the level of organized resistance. For one implication of this analysis is that struggle on the inside must deal with the same conflicts as struggle on the outside. Resisting the acting out of a foundational fantasy on ever-larger scales is one arena for action; dealing with the fantasy in personal psychical life is the other. The burden of this book is that the force of the fantasy in both areas increases simultaneously.

Predominantly, this is an economic and political argument. At another level, it is theological: as I have indicated, conceptually, the foundational fantasy parallels St Augustine's understanding of original sin. In particular, the foundational fantasy, like Augustinian original sin, is grounded in pride (narcissism in psychoanalysis) and envy (envy in psychoanalyis). Both pride and envy result from a death drive to subordinate the other, to make the other into an object, 'denying its worth before God'. Yet while there is this parallel, there is also a divergence. In Augustine's account, the sin is in us. In my account, we are in the sin. By this I mean that we humans purchase the illusion of self-containment through the foundational fantasy or original sin: there is no sense of self-containment before the fantasy takes hold (although there can be a sense of distinctness, a distinct soul). There is no sense of self-containment in that beneficent and destructive energies and affects flow between the nascent subject, its surrounding environment, and those in it. These affective energies pre-exist us; we are born into them. They bequeath to us the illusion that the subject founds the world, that the subject has dominion over it, together with the drive and desire to do away with any evidence to the contrary, chief amongst it the living, thinking other. To think we contain – in the sense of originate – the sin, or the fantasy, is to fall into a *post hoc, ergo proctor hoc* reasoning. None the less, we make that sin our own by acting in accord with its dictates. This we do to greater or less extents. My point is that the social grip of original sin is not always uniform, nor is the resistance to it.

In my account there can be more, or less, 'original sin' (which constitutes another divergence from Augustine. For him, original sin is a given). Subjects are driven by the foundational fantasy to different degrees. The difference in degree depends largely on environmental factors. That said, in no sense do I want to reduce original sin to socio-historical factors. Rather, I am making a different claim, which is that the strength of original sin is set by socio-historical circumstances. In an economy in which life and nature have less breathing space, the death drive has more. Its strength is determined by the energetic shifts wrought by technologies, from the tension of pollution to the suppression of living nature in favour of the built environment, and the correlate suppression of the body in its adaption to regimentation rather than rhythm. Depending on the strength of the death drive, the foundational fantasy will increase or decrease in force. The reason the fantasy, or sin, cannot be reduced to these circumstances is that its mythical and psychical representations predate them. As a psychical event, something akin to a Western fantasy, it occurs even in fortunate circumstances. But whether this psychical event takes hold of the bulk of a person's consciousness, let alone the course of Western history, is problematic. However, the fact that the foundational fantasy has been enacted in the West to the degree it has means that it is playing a determinate role in history. It is also plain that the force of the fantasy is stronger in the West than anywhere else, and that it is gradually making itself into a global event. It makes itself into this event by economic means, but these means of themselves are insufficient to explain the speed with which the fantasy has taken hold as a kind of mindset. We are told, often, that one of the striking features of the spread of capitalism in the third world and Eastern Europe was the rapidity with which it was embraced. 'See', goes this reasoning, 'it is only normal for people to want to have more; it is only right that they should wish to be gratified by choice and speedy service. It is after all natural for them to compete.' From this naturalizing standpoint, the rapid spread of an economic and political ideology at odds with its socialist and feudal predecessors can be explained by the eagerness with which it was desired before its advent. This explanation is both true and not true. It is true if one concedes the existence of the foundational fantasy, in so far as that fantasy is an ever-present disposition. But the explanation of a natural disposition to capitalism is also not true: it presupposes a unified psyche, a psyche entirely possessed by the foundational fantasy, without alternate strivings towards generosity and nobility of spirit.

In sum, my position here is this: by appealing to the grubby foundationalism in us all (human cupidity), capitalism gathers strength. But without an economy which made the fantasy come true (for a few), the fantasy's, and the sin's, influence over human affairs would dwindle. But this process works both ways. Psychical and contemplative resistance will also have effects; the difficulty is securing the space to clear one's mind of the egoic rubbish that bombards it in a capitalist modernity. To act kindly, let alone pray or meditate in a world in which subjective aggression roams freely is not impossible, just extraordinarily difficult. It is made more difficult by economic circumstance and daily stress. *Contra* many myths, good character is often a luxury of the rich, or those with the space and time to cease planning how to have.

That said, the influence of the subjective and social spheres upon one another should not be discounted. If the indissolubility of individual and environment is taken completely seriously, every action, every thought, has an effect. The decision not to project a moment's aggression, not to impose a negative image on the other or in other ways manipulate for subjective advantage – these decisions resist and reverse moments of objectifying aggression. As with the aggression they resist, these decisions may reverberate throughout the cosmos, like Lorenzo's butterfly. They are also the moments at which 'choice' and the individuality it is meant to reflect become real: moments in which personal distinctness manifests itself in the soup of the ego's era. If I have given no attention to individual distinctness, this is because recognizing the common connections between people, connections that work for good and ill, is more the task of the times. It does not mean that people, any more than all the elements of the natural order, lack the distinctive beauty that marks each single snowflake. It does mean that they are less likely to reveal this distinctiveness when they parrot the rhetoric which homogenizes difference in the name of the ego: a rhetoric of me and mine which makes everyone sound the same, even or especially when the chatter is about difference.

But if one can resist one's impulse to dominate in the name of the ego, how does one resist being dominated? For that matter, and crucially, is there a structural basis for resistance? These questions are related, and the relation between them depends on reasserting the claims of generational time against the megalomania of the punctual self.[2] More specifically, Marxism discerned a structural basis for resistance, wrongly, as it turned out, in the development of the productive forces; for Marx the larger scale would work towards undermining capital, by increasing working-class solidarity, amongst other things. While the theory was wrong, it has left a legacy in the form of a strong radical predisposition to seek grounds for the structural undermining of the system. It has also left a labour movement history of solidarity – a form of connection – which no modern movement of resistance should ignore.

Organized working-class action has often exemplified forms of resistance which refused to give away intelligence and direction, without assuming a subjectivity which humiliates and denigrates others as people. It has done so through the solidarity or collectivity of its members, through the opposition to individualism: an opposition which can be the best protection available to personal integrity, when it does not seek to demean that other's difference, but embraces that other's likeness. In this, it serves as a model of action for other movements; solidarity can have force without destructiveness. At the same time, that solidarity has been most real, union resistance most effective, when mind and body were not drastically separated in the industry at issue (as for instance in mining), and where the scale of action was such as to mean contact between people was other than superficial.

Keeping this in mind, I turn to the structural question. The main criticism of theories advocating an environmentally focused restructuring of the economy is their utopian nature: 'utopian', in that they may ignore the structural realities of the present. Thus, for example, Hayward argues that works on ecology have 'tended to jump too quickly from warnings of envionmental crisis to political and philo-sophical conclusions . . . oscillating between catastrophism and utopianism'.[3] Boggs[4] argues that even the more thought-ful environmentalists, such as Porritt,[5] miss 'a dialectical understanding of change' that connects the vision of the future to the economic structures of the day. 'Without this sort of linkage there can be no really efficacious practice of a *transitional phase* that involves a long and difficult shift in the nature of class and power relations'.[6] In fact huge social changes have been accomplished by spiritual and religious movements empowered by conviction. But the question of whether such movements can sustain their action effectively without a strategic, structural awareness remains.

One of the aims of this book has been to contribute to this awareness by drawing out the dialectical implications of capital's spatial expansion in relation to nature. This makes the question of economic scale paramount rather than incidental. It means that any opposition to the dominant economy of the day cannot call simply on socialism; it has to call on an alteration in scale. I discuss the question of scale in more detail elsewhere, but I note now that there is a structural economic basis for resistance in the smaller-scale economies.[7] While these may have aided megalithic capital since its inception, they can also abet its demolition. More-over, small-scale business in the advanced heartlands is not the only form of small-scale production. There is also the subsistence or 'sustenance' economy (as Gandhi renamed it) that is daily eroded in the third world.

There are some points I need to make about this susten-ance economy before returning to the structural basis for economic resistance in the West. Shiva,[8] following Gandhi, has argued that, in this economy, the labour of women is geared to the preservation of nature. Both the economic position of women, and the regard for nature's replenish-ment, are better protected by the small scale of the sustenance economy. The structural basis for resistance that still exists in India (and elsewhere) is eroded in the name of development, which confuses the question of scale with the question of technology. Needless to say, technology can be improved, and life enhanced through it, without these improvements necessitating the increase in scale which relegates women as mothers to the economic margins as it hastens the over-consumption of nature. The problem is that women in sustenance economies may be working in structures which potentially oppose the larger economic scale, but the social and political power needed to implement that opposition is lacking. This lack has to be countered in any theory and practice of transition. Let us note immediately, however, that third world women also labour under systems of public symbolization (especially religion) which denigrate women. In this their position is similar to that of Western pre-industrial women. On the one hand, both non-metropolitan and pre-industrial women have far greater economic power. On the other hand, the practical position of these women is at odds with their symbolic description as weak of intellect, passive, and so on. The written or Church record is one thing. The agency of, and recognition accorded, women off the written record is or was another. The acting out that gave the written record more credibility came later.

Historically, the economic recognition of women lacked a vocabulary in which it could be expressed. Much of the confusion in the progress-oriented thinking that accompanies foundationalism, and lends itself to the illusion that the position of women has improved, stems from the disjunction here between the visible and symbolic record and the invisible practical realm. Still more confusion results from the fact that the economic power of women who simultaneously occupied the position of mothers is occluded, because in the pre-industrial division of labour, the connection between home and workplace meant that women were (or are) economically effective at the same time as they occupied the position of mother. The position is a long way from the solitary mothers, the impoverished fixed points, discussed above (p. 144). Making the (relatively) economically empowered woman-as-mother invisible is in some ways the essence of the foundational fantasy. And while the power of the woman-as-mother was denied officially before the seventeenth century, the denial could never be as thorough-going as it is when the woman's position becomes an economically dependent one, closer to an infantile one in fact.

Today, in the third world, the marginalization of women through inappropriate technologies is the more possible precisely because of the patriarchal symbolic traditions which denied the agency of women long before this denial was acted out with capitalization. As I have stressed, feudal patriarchy could only give birth to the ego's era because it denied the mother's agency. There was no 'vocabulary' in which this agency was expressed. Any process of economic reversal from the large scale to a smaller one, any attempt at retracing the steps that led to the ego's era can only be effective in the long term if it acknowledges the maternal forces it draws on. For the same reason, in the third world today, the symbolic continuity between the theoretical denial of women, and the techno-economic practice which benefits from it, has to be broken. But attempts to break it will be ineffective without a limit on imperialism, and this takes us back to the potential political role of small businesses in the advanced heartlands of the West.

The sustenance economy is a long way from these small businesses, but the distance is less if one sees the latter as the heirs, at the level of scale, to a similar if long-departed sustenance economy in the West. Historically, to some extent, these small-scale pockets grew out of household economies in which men and women were economically interdependent. The small-scale business economy can be viewed as a mini-version of mega-capital, or a mode of production in competition with it. Pockets of small business helped the rise of large-scale capital, but later they become its victims. If the small business mode is seen as competing with capital, it can be seen as a structural and strategic basis for resistance. The sheer number of people already self-employed in this mode of production is a force in itself. It is a force that could be mobilized in opposition to the large scale, if the question of scale in business is made an explicit issue. In other words, by focusing on scale, some small-scale entrepreneurs could be called into an alliance with the other forces opposed to corporatism, such as the union movement.

Small-scale entrepreneurs constitute an unreliable class for the classical Marxist. And naturally, if they are asked to choose between large-scale capitalism and large-scale socialism, these small-scalers will be unreliable. But if asked to choose between legislation which enhances and advantages small-scale businesses, and a vague monetarism which eulogizes all competition, they would choose wisely. What follows from this is the idea of setting political limits on gain, the *appetitus divitirum infinitus*. By the economic analysis offered here, setting limits on gain is the same thing as setting limits on scale. We saw at the outset that the medieval church lost in its attempt to set limits on one form of gain. But reviving and extending that struggle to the sphere of life (captured in commodities) does not denigrate the entrepreneurial factor; it should rather limit the negative effects of large-scale competition. It should increase the opportunities for creativity for more people. By cutting back the territory of production currently occupied by the megaliths, it expands the potential opportunities for more people to join body and mind together in labour having a direct relation to their product. Moreover, to limit the scale of business in the West would be to limit automatically the power of the multi-nationals, thus limiting imperialism. It would be to implement a program in the West which assisted the third world in the preservation of its own sustenance economies. It would also be to aid the protection of the environment at the structural level. If all this is accompanied by a stress on how the denial of women, nature, and the connecting forces between them makes some blind to what they receive and what they owe, it will have more symbolic strength, a strength that depends on the unity fostered by its symbolic truth.

Of course, by no means all small-scale enterprises are environmentally desirable. The extent to which they are ecologically viable has to be considered. The point is that their scale means they are more likely to be environmentally friendly. We have seen that, to maintain the speed necessary for effective competition, large-scale capital needs to be able to bring its natural raw materials from ever-larger distances. If it is unable to do this, the close-to-hand environment has to be preserved and generational time respected.

In terms of practical programmes, setting limits on gain and scale is something that can be done through political parties, as an integral part of any attempt at distributive justice and environmental reform. To some extent, setting limits means recrediting national, or federal, boundaries, for limiting scale means aiming for self-sufficiency in restricted areas. And *contra* the revolutionary road to socialism, any such programme would mean using democracy in full awareness of the conflicts that will arise with the megaliths. But it also means using democracy with some economic resources on the side of the good. The lack of such resources has always been a problem for those advocating the peaceful parliamentary road to socialism.

To think in terms of limiting scale is to think in terms that at one level have been thoroughly thought out, by Gandhi and others. This programme does not mean turning one's back on the existing parties or states; the state itself need not be 'smaller'; it could be 'broader and thinner'.[9] The state would become thinner as it limited its alliances with the megalith; it would do this as it limited the consumption of nature, as it withdrew the unbridled political licence by which the gobbler gobbles. But for the state to do this, it obviously has to exist and be the subject of democratic contestation between parties. It can be used, just as the city can be used. Both state and city have great costs, but the first could become an agency of protection; the second the place of a gathering, a meeting ground for the opposition.

For of course there is an opposition that extends far beyond the small market and union hall. If this opposition is not known to itself, this is, in part, because the foundational fantasy splits people from one another. The splitting that secures subjective identity is replayed at all the levels on which the fantasy is acted out. This splitting obscures the common grounds for opposing the fantasy, and thus the means for uniting the fragmented opposition to it. Yet while splitting is endemic to the fantasy, and subjectivity as we know it, its force varies, just as the fantasy varies in its impact. Splitting, at present, riddles all levels of political life. To resist the urge to split, the urge to ridicule those elements of the opposition one does not identify with; this is something that is extremely difficult. The tendency to think in terms of existing binary categories is very powerful. It is especially problematic to think in terms which try to run an emphasis on holistic connection together with historical economic analysis, without giving in to the long-standing tension between them. But some days are better than others; the demons do not always win.

What this analysis does is remove the grounds that divide the opposition to various manifestations of the fantasy. It does this by symbolizing the maternal living force which is rivalled by the fantasy, and by delineating the fantasy and its acting out. Delineating the fantasy shows how common evils are intrinsically connected; this in turn permits us to symbolize connections between common goods, or the concerns of movements which, while they may be oblivious to notions of an origin that is also maternal as well as paternal, none the less *act* against various manifestations of the fantasy. Thus the stress on loving one's neighbour as oneself is aligned here with the opposition to sexism, racism, and to other projective fantasies that seize on sexual orientation as an excuse for offloading aggression. These things are allied with the opposition to any economic system that degrades human creative potentials, and takes more from than it gives back to nature. The counter-cultural stress on spiritual connection is aligned here with the union movements which struggle for rights for migrant workers, and with the struggles of different ethnic groups, and the economic battles of women and mothers, especially single mothers. Acknowledging one's indebtedness to and dependence on the extraordinary creativity of the *Deus sive Natura* is aligned here with the opposition to power over others in any form; the concern with symbolizing divinity in maternal terms[10] becomes an imperative, but it is an imperative that is aligned with the advocacy of tolerance that lends liberal vocabularies their good sense as distinct from their egoism. The intellect is allied with the living spirit, for it is the intellect's task to labour against the fixed points that block thought and the resurrection of the body. The fact that so many movements embody aspects of this alliance, the power of the life drive evident in all of them, is grounds for real optimism. Together these movements constitute an opposition to the acting out of the fantasy in all its aspects. But, at present, these movements are undermined by the fixed points of ridicule that stand between them: fixed points that divert the life drive into deathly paths. It can be said, and rightly, that the aggression against the other that secures subjectivity through these fixed points will not just go away. But this aggression can find a more suitable object; it could and should be the foundational fantasy and all its manifestations. The more the fantasy comes into focus as the common opponent, the less the opposition will be divided amongst itself.

Apart from the effects of splitting, the opposition is undermined by the imitation of the original, which makes it hard to trace the fine line between what to oppose and what to advocate. The imitation of natural logic by a constructed foundation makes it easy to confuse the question of *subjective* foundations with *any* foundations, to confuse the totalizing trend we confront with theories that appear to totalise. Making these distinctions is a matter of judgement, a necessary condition for restoring the balance disturbed by the original's imitation.

Although the process of imitation constructs a complex physical alternative world which papers over the original, and makes it hard to see the forest for the trees (or even to find a tree) this should not blind one to the existence of the original. It is true we cannot know this original with certainty. But if I am right, it may be we can learn more about the workings of the original through tracing the inverted path of the imitation. This is more likely to be so if the imitation does in fact compete with the original, so that an unconscious knowledge of the original informs the direction and content of its competitive contender. By reading the inverted path of the imitation, which is envious and fragmenting, we can deduce that the original is generous and cohering; if the imitation is repetitive, the original only makes the joke once; if the imitation seeks to abolish time, we can conclude that the original is timeless; if the imitation seeks to be everywhere at once, by instant telecommunications and most rapid transit, we deduce that the original is everywhere already. If the imitation is always trying to be something, and cares desperately for its status, the original is really something, and does not care.

Notes

1 Bernard Williams, *Ethics and the Limits of Philosophy* (London: Fontana Press, 1985), p. 46.
2 Taylor, *Sources of the Self: The Making of the Modern Identity.*
3 Tim Hayward, 'Eco-Socialism – Utopian and Scientific', *Radical Philosophy*, no. 56 (1990), pp. 2–14, p. 2 and *Ecological Thought: An Introduction* (Cambridge, MA: Blackwed Publishers, 1995).
4 Carl Boggs, 'The Green Alternative and the Struggle for a Post-Marxist Discourse', *Theory and Society*, vol. 15, no. 6 (1986), pp. 869–99.
5 Jonathon Porritt, *Seeing Green: The Politics of Ecology Explained* (Oxford: Basil Blackwell, 1984).
6 Boggs, 'The Green Alternative', p. 894.
7 Teresa Brennan, *Your Money or Your Life: The Real Third Way* (forthcoming).
8 Vandana Shiva, *Staying Alive: Women, Ecology, and Survival in India* (London: Zed Press, 1988).
9 R. W. Connell, 'The State, Gender and Sexual Politics: Theory and Appraisal', *Theory and Society*, vol. 19, no. 5 (October 1990), pp. 507–44, p. 538.
10 Chung Hyun Kyung, *Struggle to be the Sun Again: Introducing Asian Women's Theology* (Maryknoll, NY: Orbis Books, 1990). Leila Ahmed, *Women and Gender in Islam: Historical Roots of a Modern Debate* (New Haven: Yale University Press, 1992). Katie G. Cannon et.al., *God's Fierce Whimsy: Christian Feminism and Theological Education* (New York: Pilgrim Press, 1985).Ursula King (ed.), *Feminist Theology from the Third World: A Reader*

(Maryknoll, NY: Orbis Books, 1994). Kwok Pui-lan and Elizabeth Schussler Fiorenza (eds), *Women's Sacred Scriptures* (Maryknoll, NY: Orbis Books, 1998). Laura Levitt and Miriam Peskowitz (eds), *Judaism Since Gender* (New York and London: Routledge, 1997). Tamar Rudavsky, *Gender and Judaism: The Transformation of Tradition* (New York and London: New York University Press, 1995).

AFTERWORD

In part, this book is an abbreviated edition of an earlier work titled *History after Lacan*. I have dispensed with the discussion of Lacan and history, and focused on the book's principal argument on political economy. I have also added new chapters. As this edition dispenses with the chapter on Lacan and other material which suggested that the main purpose of the book was to engage with postmodern arguments on history, I wish to make one thing plain. No disrespect to Lacan (major thinker that he is) is intended here. I am simply highlighting, by process of abbreviation, that for the main part the book is about something else.

Over the years, I have received many compliments for the way I took on the foundationalist concept of history. But *History after Lacan* was more or less arguing the opposite: it was arguing for the conceptual significance of history and its importance to Lacan. The failure to make the point can be explained two ways: first, those overburdened graduate students did not read the book; second, the title was misleading. To read a title such as *History after Lacan* is to anticipate reading a certain style of book, a book with a certain theoretical market. I fondly entertained the belief that the best way to help critical theory re-engage with the economic concerns that have receded in recent debates was to address these concerns through Lacan. Lacan has purchase in critical theory, and while he is often perceived as an opponent of general theories of history (and hence a post-structuralist and postmodern thinker), the fact that he argues the other way provided a bridge from postmodernism to the general theory I wish to present. As a strategy, this had partial success. But this is a period where people are pressured by the demands of their disciplines and specialties to read only in those fields. Those who are interested in Lacan may wish to read the chapters excised here in *History after Lacan*.

This book as it stands outlines a theory of the modern economy. It constitutes one part of a three part argument: the other two parts are also outlined briefly in this book. They deal, respectively, with a psychoanalysis of femininity and the categories of thought; second, the transmission of energy and affect. Of course both topics require book length treatment, and in fact, I have published a version of the psychoanalytic argument. I am working now on the transmission of energy. As with economics, energetics is a field with relevant empirical literatures. My work on it will include a discussion of its empirical bearings. The empirical relation between the economic theory presented in *Exhausting Modernity* and the contemporary economy is discussed in a companion volume, *Your Money or Your Life: The Real Third Way* (forthcoming).

Teresa Brennan
Florida,
25 March 2000

INDEX